Also by Perla Meyers

The Peasant Kitchen

*Perla Meyers' From Market to
    Kitchen Cookbook*

The Seasonal Kitchen

BURPEE'S

AMERICAN HARVEST

COOKBOOKS

☆

THE
SPRING
GARDEN

By

Perla Meyers

A FIRESIDE BOOK
Published by Simon & Schuster Inc.
New York London Toronto Sydney Tokyo

. . . .

To Michael diBeneditto for his strong, never failing support, for his help and dedication, and for his spirited thoroughness in testing the recipes.

. . . .

Photography by Simon Metz
Food Styling by Michael diBeneditto

A FIRESIDE BOOK, published by Simon & Schuster Inc., Simon & Schuster Building, Rockefeller Center, 1230 Avenue of the Americas, New York, NY 10020.

FIRESIDE and colophon are registered trademarks of Simon & Schuster Inc.

DESIGNED BY JOEL AVIROM

Manufactured in the United States of America

10 9 8 7 6 5 4 3 2 1

Library of Congress Cataloging-in-Publication Data

Meyers, Perla.
　The spring garden/by Perla Meyers; photography by Simon Metz; food styling by Michael diBeneditto.
　　p. cm.—(Burpee's American harvest cookbooks)
　　"A Fireside book."
　　Includes index.
　　ISBN 0-671-63362-7 (pbk.): $8.95
　　1. Cookery (Vegetables)　2. Vegetable gardening.
I. W. Atlee Burpee Company.　II. Title.　III. Series:
Meyers, Perla. Burpee's American harvest cookbooks.
TX801.M493 1988
641.6′5—dc19　　　　　　　　　87-28537
　　　　　　　　　　　　　　　　　　　　CIP

I wish to thank Dean & DeLuca, Wolfman Gold, and The Silo for the use of their accessories.

Picture Credits: Burpee—7, 8, 14, 18, 24, 29, 30, 33, 48, 56, 58, 59, 60, 63, 64, 65, 71, 73, 86, 88, 89, 93, 94, 99, 100, 102, 111, 112, 114, 116, 118, 121, 126; Bettmann Archive—36, 38, 39, 66, 103; Dover Publications *Food and Drink*—10, 21, 35, 42, 44, 46, 53, 68, 77, 78, 81, 105, 107; Dover Publications *Goods and Merchandise*—28. Every effort has been made to locate and credit other artwork used in this book. If any has been overlooked, we welcome credit information which will be included in future editions.

C·O·N·T·E·N·T·S

From the time I was a small child watching over a simple garden of radishes, lettuces, and carrots, I have been in awe of the vigor and promise of each fragile seedling that pokes through the earth. When I finally grew up and had a place to start a garden of my own, I naturally sent away for my first Burpee catalog. It was a great inspiration and turned gardening into a new experience for me.

Now, come February and the latest Burpee catalog in hand, the dead of winter is far from my mind; I fill my thoughts with the coming season. This is a time when I can leisurely explore the impressive varieties of "garden classics" as well as the new and uncommon vegetables that will yield optimum flavor, variety, and the longest possible harvest. Fresh vegetables never disappoint. Perhaps that is why they play an essential part in every major cuisine. For me no meal is complete without a vegetable, whether in the main course, a soup, or a salad.

As a cook and a gardener I find the vegetable garden inspires lightly sauced pastas, vegetable-studded pizzas, deeply flavored soups, and inventive casseroles. And I know that whatever my choices, Burpee seeds will produce wonderful vegetables. That has been the Burpee guarantee for more than 100 years.

The company was founded in 1876 by W. Atlee Burpee, an 18-year-old poultry breeder whose small catalog of poultry and livestock included seeds imported from Europe. Seed sales soon dominated the business. In 1888 Burpee set up his own seed-testing station in Doylestown, Pennsylvania, and by the end of the century had one of the world's largest mail-order seed houses. Burpee is still dominant, but its impact has been even greater than its position in the seed business, for whether one gardens or not, every American has enjoyed the benefits of Burpee's unique vegetable developments. Such varieties as Fordhook bush lima beans and Golden Bantam corn are benchmarks in the history of American agriculture and standard items in the national diet. The founder's son, David Burpee, took over the company and over the years introduced the world's first hybrid tomatoes, cucumbers, and other vegetables. Burpee's Big Boy hybrid tomato, introduced in 1949, is still one of America's most popular.

Burpee seeds today are planted in millions of American gardens. The company is constantly keeping pace with our changing lifestyles, the increasing interest in home gardening, and the endless American appetite for new products. Faster maturing plants with greater resistance to disease are being bred, as well as those with shorter vines, to fit and thrive in our small suburban—and urban—gardens. Such stylish greens as arugula and radicchio, until recently encountered only in fashionable restaurants, are now available to the home gardener.

For me, the garden is a natural extension of the kitchen, and Burpee's new or improved varieties only serve to enlarge the possibilities. Along with the increased awareness in this country of all things fresh is the great inspiration of many American cooks and chefs who now have so many varieties of vegetables and herbs available to them. This cookbook series takes advantage of those current trends. The Burpee American Harvest Cookbooks are collections of carefully created recipes that look first of all to the best produce available—that which is grown and harvested by the home gardener at the peak of freshness, flavor, and goodness. These are not vegetarian cookbooks but books that look to excellent produce as the center of a dish and a meal; by their very nature they also help us celebrate seasons at the table.

Here in *The Spring Garden* are recipes based on the favorites of the season, the ones that seem to truly signal the end of the dreary time of year—asparagus, peas, spinach, the great variety of greens, for cooking and for salads, and the spring garden accents, scallions and radishes. The assortment and range, from savory soups to pasta dishes and main courses, bring the garden to the table for a season's worth of meals. I hope you enjoy cooking them as much as I've enjoyed creating them.

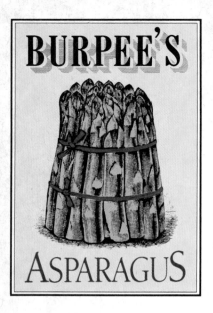

There was a time when spring was marked by the arrival of fresh asparagus at the markets. Suddenly, in mid-March, there they were—first pencil thin, then fat and juicy looking. Long before you tired of them, asparagus would again disappear for another nine months.

Today things are quite different. Asparagus are being shipped from thousands of miles away and their season has been lengthened to an average of six months. Still, the wonderful taste is at its best when the stalks are cut fresh from the garden.

When I was growing up, the asparagus season was celebrated with some reverence. Asparagus was considered a delicacy that received undivided attention as an appetizer accompanied by a well-flavored hollandaise, a mustard sauce, or a lemon mayonnaise. The asparagus we enjoyed then were snow white, a result of blanching—a gardening method by which the entire stalks are covered with soil to shield them from sun and prevent the photosynthesis that leads to the development of green pigment.

There are few spring vegetables that lend themselves to as many exciting preparations as asparagus. One of the most delicious soups I know of is an intensely flavored asparagus soup, and both hot and cold pasta dishes work beautifully with this vegetable. It is delicious sautéed with peas and diced ham (see page 14) or pickled (see page 21).

At the same time, asparagus, more than other vegetables, has the "presence" to be served by itself as an appetizer with little adornment other than melted butter. The Italian way of serving a plateful of cooked asparagus topped with fried eggs is one of the best ways to enjoy this delectable vegetable; I often serve it as a light main course along with crusty bread and some sweet butter. Although I rarely serve asparagus with the meal, I find that it makes a wonderful accompaniment to broiled salmon or poached or sautéed scallops.

Generally, asparagus needs little or no garnishes, but it also allows for a more assertive sauce, such as the Provençale Mayonnaise on page 16. Asparagus that has been blanched in advance

can be reheated by gently braising it in a little butter with a touch of fresh herbs, which creates a little light sauce.

How to prepare asparagus as well as how to cook it have been matters of controversy. Some purists claim that asparagus spears should be snapped off where they break naturally, and then need little or no peeling. I prefer to cut off one to one and one-half inches from the bottom of the stalks and then peel them halfway up with a vegetable peeler or a small sharp knife. This method allows you to enjoy the entire stalk and makes for more even cooking.

Rather than steam asparagus, I prefer to cook them in plenty of boiling salted water until just done. I tie them into small bundles of even-size spears, leaving two to three spears loose for testing. I disapprove of the currently fashionable method of serving asparagus still on the crunchy side. The spears should be cooked through—certainly not overcooked or waterlogged—but also not left raw. Once cooked, asparagus should be spread on a single or double layer of paper towels and left to cool.

S·T·O·R·A·G·E

It is best to cook asparagus the same day you pick it or buy it. I usually blanch the entire batch and serve it hot one day and chilled the next. Asparagus keeps well up to four or five days refrigerated in a plastic bag. When prepared a day ahead of time and refrigerated, it is best to bring asparagus back to room temperature since the cold kills the subtle taste of the delicious spears.

To freeze asparagus, snap about two inches off the stalks, separate the stalks according to thickness, and then blanch in boiling water, counting two minutes for the thin stalks and three to four minutes for medium ones. Or the stalks may be steamed, which usually takes another minute or two.

Asparagus, unlike most vegetables, is a hardy perennial. Once planted, however, you cannot expect to reap significant harvests for at least two years. Once established, asparagus plants can remain productive for fifteen to twenty years.

I prefer to plant one-year-old roots (available from Burpee and other sources), which become productive two years after planting, rather than sow seeds, which take an additional year. In either case planting must be done in very early spring. It will be worth your while to put extra care into preparing the soil since you literally will be laying the groundwork for years of productivity to come. Asparagus roots usually are planted in two-foot-wide trenches; a ten-foot-long trench yields about five pounds of spears each spring. Carefully follow the planting directions that accompany your roots, and be sure to incorporate lots of well-rotted manure or compost into the soil. Resist the temptation to cut any spears at all the first year, or more than just a few the second. This way plants will direct optimal energy toward developing strong, permanent root systems.

Established asparagus plants require little fuss. Each spring, use Burpee vegetable fertilizer before growth begins. Be generous with water, especially while the fernlike top growth is developing; the heavier the top growth in summer, the better the yields the following spring. A three-inch layer of straw applied to asparagus beds as a mulch will help retain soil moisture. In addition, the stalks will be cleaner and less in need of peeling.

H · A · R · V · E · S · T · I · N · G

The first asparagus can be harvested about the time that daffodils and tulips unfurl. Spears are ready when they are six to eight inches high, before any tip buds begin to open. Commercial growers use a special V-shaped asparagus knife, but this tool sometimes causes damage to underground stems. I prefer to snap off the spears, bending them sharply until they break. As the season progresses you may have to harvest daily to keep up with your most vigorous plants. The party is over when new spears are less than one-half inch in diameter.

R · E · C · I · P · E · S

Cream of Asparagus & Scallion Soup

1. Melt the butter in a heavy 3-quart casserole over low heat. Add the scallions, cover, and simmer until soft but not browned.

2. Add the flour and blend well. Add the chicken stock and asparagus stalks, bring to a boil and reduce heat. Simmer the soup, partially covered, for 30 minutes.

3. Cool and puree the soup until smooth in a food processor or blender.

4. Return the soup to the casserole, add the reserved asparagus tips, season with salt and pepper, and simmer until just tender. Add the cream and just heat through. Taste and correct the seasoning. Serve the soup hot or at room temperature garnished with a sprinkling of optional fresh dill.

V·A·R·I·A·T·I·O·N

This soup may also be served slightly chilled. You may have to add 1–2 cups of homemade chicken broth to thin out the soup. Correct the seasoning. A lovely cool touch is a garnish of 1 medium cucumber, seeded, cut in half and thinly sliced, and added to the soup just before serving.

4 tablespoons unsalted butter

16 medium scallions, trimmed of 3 inches of greens and finely minced to equal 2 cups

3 tablespoons all-purpose flour

6 cups Chicken Stock (page 41) or bouillon

1 pound fresh asparagus, trimmed, stalks peeled and cut into 1-inch pieces and tips reserved

Salt and freshly ground white pepper

½–¾ cup heavy cream

2 tablespoons finely minced fresh dill (optional)

SERVES 6

Fricassee of Asparagus, Peas & Ham

This lovely spring fricassee is a delicious accompaniment to poached eggs served on croutons of bread sautéed in olive oil.

P·R·E·P·A·R·A·T·I·O·N

---

2 pounds fresh peas (about 2 cups shelled)

2 teaspoons granulated sugar

Salt

1½ pounds thin asparagus, trimmed to 5 inches and stalks peeled

4–6 tablespoons unsalted butter

½ cup cubed smoked ham

Freshly ground black pepper

2 tablespoons finely minced fresh chives

SERVES 6

1. Place peas in a medium saucepan with water to cover. Add 1 teaspoon sugar and a pinch of salt. Bring to a boil, reduce heat, and simmer until barely tender. Drain and set aside.

2. Bring lightly salted water to a boil in a vegetable steamer. Add the asparagus spears, cover, and steam until barely tender. Remove and reserve.

3. In a large nonstick skillet melt the butter, add the ham, and cook for 1–2 minutes without browning.

4. Add the cooked peas and asparagus, sprinkle with the remaining sugar, and toss lightly for 2–3 minutes or until nicely glazed. You may need to add more butter.

5. Season with salt and pepper, sprinkle with chives, and serve hot as an appetizer.

Green Fettuccine with Asparagus Tips, Peas & Bibb Lettuce

P·R·E·P·A·R·A·T·I·O·N

1. Trim the asparagus spears. Remove the tips and reserve. Peel the stalks with a vegetable peeler and cut crosswise on the diagonal into ⅓-inch pieces. Set aside.

2. Bring lightly salted water to a boil in a vegetable steamer. Add the asparagus tips and sliced stalks, cover, and steam for 5 minutes or until just tender. Remove and set aside.

3. Add the snow peas, cover, and steam for 2 minutes. Remove and set aside.

4. Add the shelled peas to the steamer, cover, and steam for 3–4 minutes or until just tender. Remove and set aside.

5. In a heavy 10-inch skillet, melt 2 tablespoons butter over medium heat. Add the asparagus tips and stalks, snow peas, and shelled peas. Season with salt and pepper and toss in the butter for 1 minute. Remove with a slotted spoon to a side dish.

6. Add remaining butter to skillet and whisk until butter turns a hazelnut brown. Immediately add the cream, bring to a boil, and reduce by ⅓. Season with salt and pepper and set aside.

7. Bring plenty of lightly salted water to a boil in a large casserole. Add the fettuccine and cook until barely tender. Add 4 cups cold water to the casserole to stop further cooking. Drain the pasta well and reserve.

8. Bring the sauce to a simmer, add the sautéed asparagus, snow peas, and shelled peas. Add the Bibb or Boston lettuce and cook until just wilted. Add the Parmesan and fettuccine and just heat through. Taste and correct the seasoning, adding a large grinding of black pepper. Sprinkle with the minced dill and serve hot directly from the skillet. Serves 4 as a first course.

12 asparagus spears (about ½ pound)

Salt

20 snow peas (about 2½ ounces), strings removed

½ pound fresh peas, shelled to yield about ½ cup

8 tablespoons unsalted butter

Freshly ground black pepper

1 cup heavy cream

½ pound spinach fettuccine, preferably homemade

2 small heads Bibb lettuce, or hearts of 2 Boston lettuces, leaves separated, rinsed, and dried on paper towels

½ cup freshly grated Parmesan cheese

2–3 tablespoons finely minced fresh dill

SERVES 4

Bright Green Asparagus in Provençale Mayonnaise

This is a lovely mayonnaise that is equally delicious when served with steamed broccoli, sliced ripe avocados, or as a topping to a whole poached head of cauliflower.

1½ pounds fresh asparagus, peeled, steamed, and cooled

THE MAYONNAISE

2 cups tightly packed fresh spinach leaves, cooked, squeezed, and chopped

3 tablespoons finely minced scallions

3–4 tablespoons finely minced fresh parsley

2 large cloves garlic, peeled and crushed

3–4 flat anchovy fillets, finely minced

½ cup Crème Fraîche (page 55) or sour cream

1 cup Homemade Mayonnaise (page 88)

Juice of 1 large lemon

Salt and freshly ground black pepper

GARNISH

12–18 shrimp, shelled and cooked, marinated in a Garlic Vinaigrette (page 69)

2 tablespoons finely minced chives

2 hard-boiled egg yolks, sieved

SERVES 6

P·R·E·P·A·R·A·T·I·O·N

1. Combine the spinach, scallions, parsley, garlic, and anchovies in a food processor or blender with a little of the crème fraîche or sour cream. Process until smooth.

2. Add the mayonnaise, remaining crème fraîche or sour cream, and lemon juice. Process until smooth. Season with salt and a large grinding of black pepper and chill for 4–6 hours or overnight.

3. *To serve:* Place the cooked asparagus on a rectangular platter in an even layer. Spoon the sauce over the stems and garnish the sauce with the shrimp, chives, and sieved egg yolks. Serve slightly chilled.

Spring Pasta Salad with Asparagus in Emerald Mayonnaise

P·R·E·P·A·R·A·T·I·O·N

1. Bring plenty of water to a boil in a large saucepan. Add shrimp and cook until just opaque. Do not overcook. Drain and immediately run under cold water to stop further cooking. Peel and cut into ½-inch dice.

2. Place shrimp in a medium mixing bowl, drizzle with the oil and vinegar. Season with salt and pepper and bury the crushed clove of garlic among the shrimp. Cover and marinate at room temperature for 2 hours.

3. Bring plenty of lightly salted water to a boil in a large casserole. Add the pasta and cook until tender. Immediately add 2 cups cold water to stop further cooking. Drain well and transfer to a large serving bowl. Toss with 2 tablespoons vinaigrette, season with salt and pepper, and set aside until completely cool.

4. While the pasta is cooking prepare *the vegetables:* In a vegetable steamer, bring water to a boil. Add the peas, cover, and steam for 3–4 minutes or until just tender. Remove and set aside. Add the carrots and steam 2 minutes. Reserve. Add the asparagus, steam 4–5 minutes, and set aside.

5. Drain the marinated shrimp and add them together with the peas, carrots, and asparagus to the bowl of pasta.

6. In a food processor or blender combine the remaining vinaigrette, mayonnaise, dill, parsley, and chives. Process until smooth. Fold gently into the pasta, cover, and refrigerate overnight.

7. The next day, taste the pasta salad and correct the seasoning, adding a large grinding of black pepper. Serve slightly chilled.

½ pound medium shrimp

2 tablespoons olive oil, preferably extra-virgin

1 tablespoon red wine vinegar

Salt and freshly ground black pepper

1 large clove garlic, peeled and crushed

½ pound imported tricolor elbow pasta or other small pasta

1 recipe Provençale Vinaigrette (page 79)

½ pound fresh peas, shelled to yield about ½ cup

1 medium carrot, trimmed, peeled, and thinly sliced

¾ pound asparagus, trimmed, stalks peeled and cut into ½-inch pieces

2 tablespoons Homemade Mayonnaise (page 88)

2 tablespoons finely minced fresh dill

2 tablespoons finely minced fresh parsley

2 tablespoons finely minced fresh chives

SERVES 6–8

THE CREPE BATTER

1 cup milk

1 cup water

4 large eggs

1½ cups all-purpose flour

1 teaspoon granulated sugar

1 cup cooked corn kernels

1 teaspoon finely diced jalapeño pepper (optional)

Salt and freshly ground white pepper

Pinch of cayenne pepper

4 tablespoons unsalted butter, melted

THE SALSA

2 large ripe tomatoes, seeded and chopped, or 1 cup home-canned tomatoes, drained and chopped

2 tablespoons finely minced red onion

2 large cloves garlic, peeled and finely minced

1 large green chili pepper, roasted, peeled (page 19), and chopped

2 tablespoons finely minced fresh cilantro (coriander)

Juice of 1 lime

4 tablespoons olive oil, preferably extra-virgin

Salt and freshly ground black pepper

Tomatoes do not need to be wrapped in damp towels; just set aside to cool and then peel.

THE ASPARAGUS

36–48 thin fresh asparagus spears, trimmed to 5 inches and stalks peeled

Salt

8–10 tablespoons unsalted butter

GARNISH

Sprigs of fresh cilantro (coriander)

SERVES 6–8

Corn Crepes with
Steamed Asparagus & Spicy Salsa

P·R·E·P·A·R·A·T·I·O·N

1. Start by making *the crepe batter*: In a large mixing bowl, combine the milk, water, eggs, flour, and sugar. Whisk until well blended. Fold in the cooked corn and optional jalapeño pepper. Season with salt, pepper, and cayenne. Add the melted butter and let the batter rest at room temperature for 2 hours.

2. While the batter is resting, prepare *the salsa*: Combine the tomatoes, onion, garlic, chili pepper, cilantro, lime juice, and olive oil in a medium bowl. Season with salt and pepper and set aside.

3. *The asparagus*: Bring plenty of lightly salted water to a boil in a vegetable steamer. Add the asparagus, cover, and steam for 3–4 minutes or until just tender. Remove and keep warm.

4. *The crepes*: Melt 2 teaspoons butter in an 8-inch nonstick skillet over medium-high heat. Add 3–4 tablespoons batter and turn the skillet, tilting so that the batter coats the bottom of the pan evenly. Cook for 1 minute or until bottom of crepe is lightly browned. Turn and cook for 30 seconds longer. Transfer to a platter and keep warm. Continue making crepes using 1–2 teaspoons butter for each.

5. *To serve*: Place 2–3 asparagus spears on each crepe. Fold the crepes over to enclose the asparagus and serve about 2 crepes per person, each with a dollop of spicy salsa and a sprig of fresh cilantro.

ROASTED RED OR GREEN PEPPERS

Peppers can be roasted both indoors and outdoors. When roasting indoors, place over a medium-high gas flame or directly on electric coils until blackened and charred on all sides. For outdoors, peppers should be placed directly over hot coals. Wrap peppers in damp paper towels until cool enough to handle. To peel, run peppers under cold water and remove all skin. Core and seed. Note: When working with hot peppers, wash hands thoroughly afterward or wear rubber gloves.

Pasta Printannier with Sautéed Sliced Chicken Breasts

P·R·E·P·A·R·A·T·I·O·N

1 pound fresh asparagus, trimmed
Salt
8 tablespoons unsalted butter
1¼ cups heavy cream
1 recipe Beurre Manié (below)
   (optional)
Freshly ground white pepper
1 whole chicken breast, boned,
   skinned, and cut in half
Juice of ½ lemon
¾ pound fresh fettuccine,
   preferably homemade

GARNISH

Sprigs of Italian parsley

SERVES 4–6

BEURRE MANIÉ

Combine 1 tablespoon soft, unsalted
butter with 1 tablespoon all-purpose
flour in small bowl. Work mixture
with fork until smooth. Chill until
ready to use. Recipe can be tripled or
quadrupled (or made in large
quantities).

1. Remove the asparagus tips and set aside. Peel the stalks with a vegetable peeler and cut crosswise into ½-inch pieces.

2. Bring lightly salted water to a boil in a vegetable steamer, add the asparagus tips and stalks, cover, and steam for 4–5 minutes or until tender. Run under cold water to stop further cooking and drain on paper towels. Reserve.

3. In a large heavy skillet, melt 6 tablespoons butter over medium heat and whisk until a light hazelnut brown. Immediately add the heavy cream and whisk until well blended. Add a bit of the optional beurre manié. Reduce by ⅓. Season with salt and pepper to taste, add the reserved tips and stalks, and keep warm.

4. Dry the chicken breasts thoroughly on paper towels.

5. Heat the remaining butter in a heavy nonstick skillet over medium to medium-high heat. Add the chicken and cook until crisp and nicely browned on one side, about 3 minutes. Turn, reduce heat, and sauté until just done, about 3–4 minutes. The chicken should still be a bit pink inside. Sprinkle with lemon juice and season with salt and pepper, cover, and keep warm.

6. Bring plenty of lightly salted water to a boil in a large casserole. Add the fettuccine and cook until just tender. Immediately add 2 cups cold water to the casserole to stop further cooking and drain thoroughly.

7. Add the fettuccine to the skillet with the asparagus sauce and toss to just heat through. Taste and correct the seasoning.

8. Cut the chicken breasts crosswise on the diagonal into ¼-inch slices.

9. To serve, divide the pasta among 4–6 dinner plates. Place 3–4 slices of chicken in the center of each portion and garnish with a sprig of Italian parsley. Serve at once.

V·A·R·I·A·T·I·O·N

You may also add 2–3 tablespoons finely minced fresh chives to the asparagus sauce.

Ginger Pickled Asparagus

P·R·E·P·A·R·A·T·I·O·N
---

1. Place the asparagus pieces in a medium mixing bowl and set aside.

2. In a medium saucepan combine the rice vinegar, sugar, salt, and ginger. Bring slowly to a boil over medium heat and stir until sugar has dissolved.

3. Pour the hot syrup over the asparagus and let cool completely. Pack the asparagus in a pint jar, pour the liquid over, including the ginger slices, cover tightly, and refrigerate overnight. The asparagus will keep for up to 5–6 weeks in the refrigerator.

R·E·M·A·R·K·S

This recipe can easily be doubled, tripled, etc., and may also be "packed." In this case process the asparagus in covered jars for 10 minutes in a boiling water bath. Cool, check lids, and store in a cool place.

1 pound asparagus, peeled, trimmed and cut into 1½-inch lengths
1 cup rice wine vinegar
½ cup granulated sugar
½ teaspoon salt
2 slices fresh gingerroot, ⅛-inch thick and each about the size of a quarter

MAKES 1 PINT

Creamy Pilaf of Rice with Asparagus, Lemon & Dill

12 asparagus spears, trimmed
Salt
2 tablespoons freshly squeezed
  lemon juice
2 large egg yolks
½ cup heavy cream
½ cup freshly grated Parmesan
  cheese
2 tablespoons unsalted butter
1 small onion, peeled and finely
  minced
1½ cups rice, preferably Italian
  style
Freshly ground white pepper
3¾ cups Chicken Stock (page 41)
  or bouillon
2–4 tablespoons unsalted butter
  (optional)

GARNISH

2 tablespoons finely minced fresh
  dill

SERVES 6

P·R·E·P·A·R·A·T·I·O·N

1. Peel the asparagus stalks and cut into ½-inch pieces. Place in a saucepan with lightly salted water to cover and set over high heat. Bring to a boil, reduce heat, and cook until tender. Drain and set aside.

2. In a small bowl, combine the lemon juice, egg yolks, cream, and Parmesan cheese. Whisk until well blended. Reserve.

3. Melt the butter in a heavy 3-quart casserole. Add the onion and cook over low heat until soft but not browned. Add the rice and stir to coat with the butter.

4. Gently fold in the asparagus and season with salt and pepper.

5. Add the chicken stock, bring to a boil, reduce heat, and cover tightly. Simmer for 25–30 minutes or until rice is tender. Fold in the lemon juice mixture and optional butter gently with two forks. Taste and correct the seasoning. Sprinkle with dill and serve directly from the casserole.

R·E·M·A·R·K·S

It is best not to use converted rice since it will not absorb all the broth, resulting in a runny instead of creamy pilaf.

Spring Asparagus Soup
with Peas & Lettuce

P·R·E·P·A·R·A·T·I·O·N

1. Cut off the tips of the asparagus with a sharp knife and set aside. Slice the peeled stalks into ½-inch pieces and reserve.

2. In a 4-quart casserole, bring the chicken stock to a boil. Add the diced stalks, reduce heat, and simmer, partially covered, for 20 minutes or until very tender.

3. Strain the broth through a colander into a large bowl. Transfer the cooked stalks to a food processor or blender, together with ¼ cup broth, and puree until very smooth.

4. Whisk the asparagus puree into the remaining broth and reserve.

5. Add the butter to the casserole and melt over medium heat. Whisk in the flour and cook for 2 minutes without browning. Add the asparagus broth, all at once, and whisk constantly until the broth comes to a boil. Whisk in the heavy cream, season with salt and pepper, reduce heat, and simmer for 10 minutes.

6. Add the reserved asparagus tips and cook for 5 minutes or until just tender.

7. Add the peas and lettuce and cook until lettuce just wilts. Taste and correct the seasoning. Serve hot in individual soup bowls, garnished with tiny leaves of mint, dill, or tarragon.

1 pound fresh asparagus, trimmed and stalks peeled
6 cups Chicken Stock (page 41)
4 tablespoons unsalted butter
2½ tablespoons all-purpose flour
½–¾ cup heavy cream
Salt and freshly ground white pepper
½ cup cooked peas
1 heart Boston lettuce, separated into leaves

GARNISH

Tiny leaves of fresh mint, dill, or tarragon

SERVES 6

BURPEE'S

BEETS

For anyone who has ever strolled through a Saturday morning market in the hill towns of Provence, the sight of perfectly shaped baked beets glistening in the sun is hard to forget. There they are, a deep rich red, ready to use without further preparation.

Unfortunately, the French and Italian custom of selling already cooked beets has not been adopted by American markets, so cooks here have to plan ahead. But fresh beets are worth the somewhat lengthy cooking time, for this is a vegetable that can practically double as a fruit. Full of flavor, naturally sweet, and with a color so unique and beautiful, beets stand in a class by themselves among other root crops.

Because beets like moisture and cool temperatures, they are even more popular in northern climates. In Scandinavia cooks have created wonderful dishes with beets as the key ingredient, often combining them with apples and a sweet lemon dressing. Throughout northern and central Europe a beet, herring, and potato salad (see page 32) is a classic preparation popular both in restaurants and typical homes.

Store-bought beets tend to be large and past their prime, rendering this vegetable tough, woody, and extremely slow to cook. But when homegrown and cooked fresh, beets are deliciously sweet, slightly crisp, and good in hot or cold preparations. Beets do work best in certain combinations—particularly with such other vegetables as cucumbers, new potatoes, cabbage, and crisp salad greens. Because of their assertive color, which tends to bleed, beets should be used with ingredients and vegetables that look attractive when suddenly colored red.

Growing your own beets is extremely rewarding. I have tried varieties that are rarely available commercially and now grow the apricot-colored Burpee's Golden Beet, which is even sweeter than the red beet but does not bleed. It is quite attractive sautéed, either with a sprinkling of minced dill or as a garnish to a mixed green salad tossed in sweet honey and lemon dressing. The golden roots are especially good when picked young as "baby" beets, and the greens are better for cooking than those of the red varieties. I

use the greens for a quick stir-fry or gently stewed in a touch of butter with a light enrichment of sour cream and a sprinkling of dill.

Other fine varieties include Cylindra, a cylindrical beet that is perfect for slicing; Lutz Green Leaf, Winter Keeper, an all-purpose beet whose roots store exceptionally well; and Little Ball, a natural baby or miniature beet. Of course, any beet picked quite young can serve as a "baby." Use the little jewel-like roots for pickling whole or as a garnish to a roast duck or a sweet-and-sour beet sauce. Except for borschts, in which beets must be grated raw, all red beets must be cooked unpeeled with as much as an inch of their tops left on.

Although they take much longer to cook, baked beets retain much more taste and crispness than beets cooked in water. Tiny garden-fresh beets can be steamed, but I usually prefer cooking them in lightly salted boiling water and test them for doneness with the tip of a sharp knife. Once cooked and cool, the skins will slip right off and the beets are ready to use in flavorful salads, soups, and as a hot vegetable enhanced by a sprinkling of herbs. Although the brilliant red color of beets takes over whenever they are combined with other vegetables, they work well in either hot or cold preparations, with Belgian endives, cucumbers, potatoes, and Swiss chard.

It is well worth pickling your own beets if you have garden surplus. Even though pickled beets are readily available, I find that my own have a better texture—and they are fun to make. The Viennese pickled beets on page 31 are easy to prepare and can be served the very next day. Traditionally, they were an accompaniment to boiled beef, but are equally good with a boiled smoked tongue, a roast loin of pork, or a roast beef with a side dish of creamy horseradish sauce.

S·T·O·R·A·G·E

Beets can be stored successfully in the refrigerator for up to two weeks. Remove their greens, leaving one inch of the tops attached, and then place the roots in perforated plastic bags. Cooked beets will keep for four or five days. Although they may start to shrivel, their taste will not be affected. To prepare beets for freezing, cook them unpeeled and with an inch of their tops attached, until tender. Slip off the skins and pack them whole, sliced, or cubed in well-sealed plastic bags. They keep for four to six months.

G · A · R · D · E · N · I · N · G

The faster beets grow the better they generally taste. This is why I spend some extra time conditioning the earth to create the rich yet loose loam in which this root crop truly flourishes. Once planted in the right stuff, beets go on their merry way with little attention from the gardener.

I start sowing seeds in early spring, as soon as the ground becomes workable, and make additional sowings at three-week intervals, stopping two months before the expected arrival of fall frost. This way I have a season-long supply of young and tender roots. Because plants are hardy enough to withstand light frost, harvesting can continue far into autumn.

Beets are particularly sensitive to acidic soil, so be sure to dig in some ground limestone if the pH level is below 6.0. Just before sowing, spade or rototill the planting bed to a depth of at least eight inches, taking care to rake away any unearthed stones.

Open a seed packet of beets and what you see are "seedballs," each of which contains several seeds. Clusters of seedlings will arise from the planted seedballs, and you should promptly thin out all but the strongest seedlings from each cluster. Provide enough water during hot spells to keep beet foliage from wilting. Without plenty of water, the roots will become tough.

H · A · R · V · E · S · T · I · N · G

Beets are ready to be picked seven to eight weeks after sowing. It is best not to delay because if left in the ground the roots become

tough and woody. I check for size by pushing aside some soil by hand. If the root tops are two inches or more across, I pull them up. Do not use a trowel or other sharp tool since beet skins puncture easily, ruining the root as a kitchen vegetable.

Beet & Cucumber Salad in Sweet Mustard Vinaigrette

1. Cut the beets into ½-inch dice and place in a salad bowl.

2. Peel the cucumbers and cut into ½-inch dice. Add to the salad bowl together with the optional cheese. Set aside.

3. Combine lemon juice, sugar, mustard, dill, and scallions in a small bowl. Add the olive oil and whisk the dressing until well blended and smooth. Season with salt and pepper. Add the dressing to the beet and cucumber salad and toss gently. Chill for 4–6 hours before serving. Serve slightly chilled, accompanied by thinly sliced buttered pumpernickel bread.

4–5 medium beets (about 1 pound), cooked and peeled

1 pound small cucumbers or 1 large burpless cucumber

⅓ cup diced Swiss or Gruyère cheese (optional)

Juice of 1 large lemon

2 teaspoons granulated sugar

1 tablespoon Dijon mustard

3 tablespoons finely minced fresh dill

3 tablespoons finely minced scallions

5 tablespoons olive oil

Salt and freshly ground black pepper

SERVES 4–5

Fried Beets & Red Onions with Soy & Lime Dipping Sauce

P·R·E·P·A·R·A·T·I·O·N

THE BATTER

1¼ cups cake flour
1 cup water
1 tablespoon corn oil
1 teaspoon baking powder
½ teaspoon salt

THE DIPPING SAUCE

2 tablespoons thin soy sauce
4 tablespoons water
2 teaspoons freshly squeezed lime juice
1 medium clove garlic, peeled and mashed in a garlic press
1 small piece fresh gingerroot, peeled and mashed in a garlic press
¼ teaspoon crushed red pepper flakes
2 teaspoons granulated sugar
1 tablespoon finely minced scallions

THE VEGETABLES

4 cups corn oil for deep-frying
2 medium beets (about 12 ounces), cooked, peeled, and cut into ⅛-inch-thick slices
1 medium red onion, peeled, cut into ¼-inch-thick slices, and separated into rings
Coarse salt

SERVES 4–6

1. Combine all the ingredients for the batter in a large mixing bowl and whisk until well blended. Let the batter rest for 2 hours.

2. Combine all the ingredients for the dipping sauce in a small bowl and set aside.

3. Heat the corn oil in a large saucepan to register 375° on a candy thermometer. Dip beet slices and rings of onion into the batter, letting the excess drip off. Add to the hot oil a few at a time and cook until golden brown on one side. Turn and continue cooking again until crisp and golden brown.

4. Transfer with a slotted spoon to a double layer of paper towels to drain. Continue frying the remaining beets and onions in the same manner. Serve hot, sprinkled with coarse salt and with dipping sauce on the side.

Cream of Beet & Sour Cream Soup

1. In a medium casserole, bring lightly salted water to a boil. Add the beets, reduce heat, partially cover, and cook for 45 minutes or until tender when pierced with the tip of a sharp knife. Drain the beets and peel. Trim and cut into ¼-inch dice. Reserve 1 cup diced beets separately.

2. Place the remaining diced beets in a food processor. Add 1 cup of the stock and puree until smooth. Set aside.

3. In a heavy 4-quart casserole, melt the butter over medium heat. Add the flour and cook, whisking constantly for 1–2 minutes without browning. Add the remaining stock all at once and whisk until smooth. Bring to a boil, whisk in the pureed beets, and season with salt and pepper. Reduce heat, partially cover, and simmer 20 minutes.

4. Add the reserved 1 cup diced beets, sour cream, and lemon juice. Taste and correct the seasoning. Cook for 10 minutes longer without letting it come to a boil. Add the mint. Serve hot, ladled into individual soup bowls. Garnish each with a dollop of sour cream and a sprig of mint.

R·E·M·A·R·K·S

You may substitute dill for the mint.

Salt
4–5 medium fresh beets, trimmed of all but 2 inches of greens, roots attached
6 cups Chicken Stock (see page 41) or bouillon
4 tablespoons unsalted butter
2 tablespoons all-purpose flour
Freshly ground white pepper
1 cup sour cream
Juice of 1 lemon
2–3 tablespoons finely minced fresh mint

GARNISH (OPTIONAL)

Bowl of sour cream
Sprigs of fresh mint

SERVES 6

PICKLED BEETS

Cut 8 medium-sized cooked beets into ¼-inch slices. Divide between two 2-pint jars, add a sprig of fresh dill to each jar, and set aside. In a saucepan, combine 1 cup cider vinegar, 1 teaspoon salt, ¼ cup sugar, 5 whole black peppercorns, 1 teaspoon pickling spice, 1 bay leaf and 1 cup beet cooking liquid. Bring to a boil and simmer for 5 minutes. Pour over the beets, cover tightly and refrigerate 10 days before serving.

Viennese Beet Salad

Here is a salad that is popular throughout central Europe and Scandinavia. At home, my mother used to serve it as a light main course accompanied by steamed and buttered new potatoes. The chilled salad and hot potatoes is a wonderful combination.

P · R · E · P · A · R · A · T · I · O · N
---

1. Cut the beets and apple into ½-inch dice and combine with herring in a salad bowl and set aside.

2. Combine the sour cream, horseradish, vinegar, and scallions in a small bowl and whisk until well blended. Season with salt and pepper and spoon the dressing over the beet mixture and toss gently. Add the optional walnuts and let the salad marinate for 2–4 hours before serving.

3. Serve the salad chilled, garnished with sprigs of dill and buttered new potatoes.

4 medium beets (about 1 pound),
   cooked and peeled
1 medium apple, peeled and cored
8 ounces herring tidbits, drained
8 ounces sour cream
1 teaspoon mild horseradish
1 teaspoon red wine vinegar
3 tablespoons finely minced
   scallions, white part only
Salt and freshly ground black
   pepper
⅓ cup walnut pieces (optional)

GARNISH

Sprigs of fresh dill
12–14 tiny new potatoes, steamed
   and buttered

SERVES 6

Beet & Tuna Salad in Parsley Vinaigrette

P·R·E·P·A·R·A·T·I·O·N

1. In a large salad bowl combine the beets, white beans, tuna, onion, and capers. Set aside.

2. In a food processor or blender, finely mince the parsley. Add the vinegar, olive oil, and salt and pepper to taste, and process the dressing until smooth. Crush the garlic through a garlic press and add to the dressing.

3. Pour the dressing over the salad and toss gently. Chill for 4–6 hours before serving.

4. Bring the salad back to room temperature, taste and correct the seasoning. The salad may need a large grinding of pepper and a little additional vinegar. Serve accompanied by thin slices of buttered black bread.

4 medium beets (about 1 pound), cooked, peeled, and cut into ½-inch cubes

3 cups cooked white beans, preferably Great Northern

1 can (6½ ounces) light tuna, drained

3 tablespoons finely diced red onion

2 tablespoons tiny capers, drained

½ cup fresh parsley leaves

2–3 tablespoons red wine vinegar, preferably sherry

6–8 tablespoons olive oil, preferably extra-virgin

Coarse salt and freshly ground black pepper

1 medium clove garlic, peeled

SERVES 4–6

Sweet & Sour Beets with Swiss Chard

Here is one of my favorite spring vegetable dishes. The natural beetlike taste of chard is combined with diced cooked beets and simmered with some cream in a delicious sweet-and-sour sauce. I often serve this dish as a starter to a meal, but it makes an unusual accompaniment to all poultry and veal preparations.

3 cups Swiss chard ribs, cut into
  pieces ½ by 1¼ inches
1¼ pounds small beets, unpeeled
  and trimmed
Salt
3–4 teaspoons red wine vinegar
¾–1 cup heavy cream
4 tablespoons unsalted butter
3–4 teaspoons granulated sugar
Freshly ground black pepper

SERVES 4–6

P·R·E·P·A·R·A·T·I·O·N

1. Bring lightly salted water to a boil in a large casserole. Drop in the chard ribs; when the water returns to the boil, boil for 3 minutes. Drain the ribs in a colander, refresh immediately under cold water, and set aside.

2. Again, bring lightly salted water to a boil in the casserole. Add the beets, reduce heat, and simmer, covered, for 25–30 minutes or until tender.

3. Drain the beets and when cool enough to handle, peel (the skin will come right off). Cut into sticks, ½ by ½ by 1¼ inches, and set aside.

4. In a small bowl combine 3 teaspoons vinegar with the cream. Stir until just blended and reserve.

5. Melt the butter in a large skillet over medium heat. Add the beets and cook for 2 minutes, tossing the beets in the butter. Sprinkle with 3 teaspoons of the sugar and cook for 1 minute longer, shaking the pan back and forth to glaze the beets. Season with salt and pepper.

6. Add the vinegar/cream mixture, bring to a boil, and cook until the cream is well reduced and heavily coats the beets.

7. Reduce heat to low, add the Swiss chard ribs to the skillet, and fold into the beet mixture. Cook for 1 minute or until the Swiss chard is just heated through. Taste and correct the seasoning, adding the remaining vinegar and/or sugar if necessary and a large grinding of black pepper. Serve hot or at room temperature.

Braised Beets à la Crème

P·R·E·P·A·R·A·T·I·O·N

1. In a large skillet, melt the butter over low heat. Add the beets and sauté for 3–4 minutes, constantly shaking the pan back and forth to coat the beets evenly with the butter. Season with salt and pepper.

2. Add the cream, bring to a boil, and cook until the cream is well reduced and heavily coats the beets. Be careful not to burn the pan juices.

3. Add the chives and dill. Fold the mixture gently and simmer the beets over the lowest possible heat setting for another 3–4 minutes. Taste and correct the seasoning, adding drops of lemon juice to taste and a large grinding of pepper. Serve hot.

4 tablespoons unsalted butter

2 pounds beets, cooked, peeled, and cut into ¼-inch-thick matchsticks

Salt and freshly ground white pepper

½–¾ cup heavy cream

2–3 tablespoons finely minced fresh chives

2–3 tablespoons finely minced fresh dill

Drops of lemon juice to taste

SERVES 6

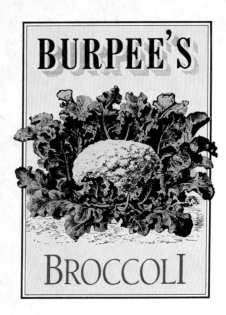

BURPEE'S

BROCCOLI

Broccoli is considered a new vegetable in the United States because it has gained wide popularity only in the last twenty years, but it has been around for centuries. Broccoli belongs to the cabbage family and is a close relative of the cauliflower. But while cauliflower, a wonderful "vintage" vegetable, enjoys only moderate popularity, its green relative now is in great demand.

Of all supermarket vegetables, broccoli is by far the best and, moreover, is available fresh and crisp-looking in the winter months when the choices are few and a green vegetable is most needed. The garden-grown vegetable is superior, however, providing florets as well as stalks tender enough for use in the kitchen.

Although everyone seems to agree that broccoli is delicious and easy to prepare, few cooks prepare it with the kind of creativity that this great vegetable deserves. Broccoli is so versatile that it works beautifully as a hot vegetable or chilled—it is a lovely addition to both hot pasta dishes and the cold Broccoli & Tuna Salad on page 44. Pureed broccoli takes on quite a different character; I love its creamy texture in a soup or molded into timbale molds. The raw stalk, finely sliced, is a superb addition to the salad bowl or can be served along with other garden vegetables and a tangy dip. Together with young peas, cooked broccoli florets are a pretty and flavorful addition to a saffron-flavored pilaf (see page 45). And when accompanied by a well-flavored mustard vinaigrette, broccoli can be served, just like asparagus, as a starter to a meal or as a separate vegetable course.

Broccoli is wonderful in Oriental preparations. It can be stir-fried and combined with shiitake mushrooms, bean sprouts, and snow peas. A touch of minced garlic and ginger plus a sprinkling of soy sauce completes a quick, spur of the moment dish that I find a most satisfying accompaniment to grilled chicken, broiled fish, or barbecued ribs.

Blanching or steaming broccoli is another matter. The key to success is to peel the stalks with a vegetable peeler or a sharp paring knife. I usually remove all the leaves, trim the stalks, and

QUICK TOMATO SAUCE

In a heavy saucepan heat 3 tablespoons olive oil; add 2 medium onions finely minced together with 2 large cloves garlic. Cook until soft. Add 4 pounds canned or home-canned Italian plum tomatoes drained together with 1 teaspoon granulated sugar and 1 sprig each thyme and oregano. Season with salt and pepper. Simmer covered for 45 minutes. Puree in food processor and correct seasonings.

Variations:
For a spicy flavor add 1 hot dried chili pepper to the oil. You may also add ½ cup basil leaves to the mixture 5 minutes before end of cooking.

if they are large, cut them lengthwise all the way through the florets into two or three pieces of equal size. To avoid overcooking broccoli, you should trim away all but 1½ inches of the stalks. If the stalks are fresh, crisp and not woody, they can be scraped, then sliced crosswise into ½-inch slices and served cooked or stir-fried. Or use them raw in Sliced Broccoli & Carrot Pickles (see page 40). If the stems seem somewhat woody and hollow, I discard all but an inch. Once peeled, the stalks will cook in the same time as the florets.

Although steaming broccoli is a popular method, I prefer cooking it in plenty of lightly salted water for three to four minutes or until the stalks can be pierced with the tip of a sharp knife. Once cooked, broccoli can be braised in a little butter for additional flavoring, or sprinkled with fruity olive oil and some red wine vinegar if it is to be used in a salad. Steaming, I have found, takes somewhat longer, and if the stalks are crowded, the florets tend to lose their bright green color and turn yellow.

For cooking in advance I find that the braising method on page 41 is by far the most successful because you can then reheat the vegetable in the skillet in which it has cooked. A broccoli puree is another excellent method for cooking broccoli in advance. You can keep the puree in the top container of a double boiler until serving time and enrich it at the last minute with two to three tablespoons of butter.

S · T · O · R · A · G · E

Broccoli stores well in a plastic bag for up to a week. For longer storage, make a broccoli puree and refrigerate it in a plastic freezer container. You can easily heat the puree right in its container in a water bath placed over low heat.

G · A · R · D · E · N · I · N · G

Adding to broccoli's popularity is the fact that it is remarkably easy to grow and wonderfully productive. Six to twelve plants will suffice for most families. Because maturing florets prefer cool weather, it is best to plant broccoli in very early spring for a late-spring harvest, and again in early to midsummer for harvests during fall. If you live in southern California or the Deep South, you can make plantings in September for good winter picking. In the North, if you want to pick broccoli as early in spring as possible, start the seed indoors about six weeks before the last predictable heavy frost.

Some broccoli varieties produce a single magnificent head and ripen all at once. I prefer varieties such as Green Goliath that offer a long harvest season; central heads, after picking, are followed for about a month by lots of harvestable side shoots. Exceptional Bonanza Hybrid boasts side shoots up to five inches across plus a head as broad as the largest single-headed varieties.

As a precaution against diseases that affect the entire cabbage family, do not plant broccoli in spots where any cole crops grew the previous year.

H · A · R · V · E · S · T · I · N · G

When in doubt, err on the side of harvesting early. Ideally, broccoli should be picked before the tight clusters of green buds begin to open and show yellow. Use a sharp knife to cut the stems. To promote continuous production of side shoots, I leave the base of harvested shoots on the plant rather than cutting them back to the main stem. Be sure to remove any spindly side shoots to prevent them from going to seed.

Sliced Broccoli & Carrot Pickles

P · R · E · P · A · R · A · T · I · O · N

½ pound broccoli stalks, peeled and cut crosswise into ⅛-inch-thick slices

2 medium carrots, trimmed, peeled, and cut crosswise into ⅛-inch slices

6 tablespoons olive oil, preferably extra-virgin

2 tablespoons red wine vinegar

½ teaspoon dried oregano

¾ teaspoon salt

Freshly ground black pepper

2 medium cloves garlic, peeled and crushed

SERVES 6

1. In a medium mixing bowl, combine the broccoli and carrot slices. Add the oil, vinegar, oregano, salt, and pepper. Toss well and bury the garlic cloves among the vegetables. Cover and refrigerate for 24 hours, turning the vegetables often in the marinade.

2. Remove the broccoli and carrots from the refrigerator 20 minutes before serving. Drain well and discard the garlic cloves. Taste and correct the seasoning and serve at room temperature on a shallow plate with toothpicks as part of an hors d'oeuvre table.

Braised Broccoli with Garlic

P·R·E·P·A·R·A·T·I·O·N

1. Trim the broccoli stalks, removing all leaves. Peel stalks with a vegetable peeler and cut crosswise into ½-inch slices. Separate the tops into florets about ¾ inch in diameter.

2. In a heavy 10-inch skillet, heat the olive oil over medium heat. Add the broccoli stems together with the garlic cloves and cook for 1–2 minutes, stirring often. Add the florets and the chicken stock. Season with salt and pepper. Bring to a boil, cover, reduce heat, and simmer for 10 minutes or until just tender. Taste and correct the seasoning. Serve at once.

V·A·R·I·A·T·I·O·N

Core, seed, and thinly slice a large red bell pepper and sauté in the olive oil (before adding the broccoli stems) for 1–2 minutes, or until just tender. Season with salt and pepper. Remove from the skillet and set aside. Continue with recipe, adding the sautéed red pepper to the finished broccoli dish. Toss to heat through.

1 large bunch broccoli (about 1½ pounds)

⅓ cup olive oil, preferably extra-virgin

2 large cloves garlic, peeled and thinly sliced

⅓ cup Chicken Stock (below) or bouillon

Salt and freshly ground black pepper

SERVES 4–6

CHICKEN STOCK

In large casserole, combine two 3-pound chickens cut in eight pieces, 2 scraped carrots, 2 stalks celery, 2 leeks, and 3 to 4 sprigs Italian parsley. Add 12 cups cold water. Season with a teaspoon salt. Bring to a boil, reduce heat, and simmer for 1 hour and 30 minutes. Strain stock. Chill overnight. The next day, skim all fat. Bring back to a boil. Cool and refrigerate or freeze in covered jars. Makes 3 quarts.

Variations: For beef or veal stock, substitute 4 to 5 pounds of meaty beef bones for chicken. You may also use a combination of veal and beef or veal and chicken, which will give the stock a more gelatinous consistency.

Steamed Broccoli with Scallion & Sesame Mayonnaise

1 large bunch broccoli (about 1
   pound), trimmed of all leaves

Salt

¼ cup peanut oil

¼ cup olive oil

1 tablespoon sesame oil

1 large egg

1 large egg yolk

1 tablespoon rice wine vinegar or
   cider vinegar

Freshly ground white pepper

Pinch of cayenne pepper

1 small clove garlic, peeled and
   mashed

3 tablespoons finely minced
   scallions

1 tablespoon sesame seeds, lightly
   toasted

Drops of lemon juice to taste

SERVES 6

P·R·E·P·A·R·A·T·I·O·N

1. Trim off all but 1½ inches of broccoli stems and discard. Separate the tops into florets and reserve.

2. Bring plenty of water to a boil in a vegetable steamer. Add the broccoli florets, season lightly with salt, cover, and steam for 2 minutes. Remove and set aside to cool.

3. Combine the peanut, olive, and sesame oil in a 1-cup liquid measure and reserve.

4. In the container of a blender combine the egg, egg yolk, rice vinegar, salt, pepper, and pinch of cayenne. Blend at high speed for 30 seconds, then with the blender still at top speed start adding the oils by droplets. As the mayonnaise begins to thicken add the remaining oil in a slow, steady stream until creamy and smooth. The consistency should be saucelike rather than that of commercial mayonnaise.

5. Add the garlic, scallions, and sesame seeds. Taste and correct the seasoning, adding drops of lemon juice to taste.

6. Serve at room temperature with the broccoli arranged on a serving platter and the mayonnaise on the side.

Pasta with Broccoli in Garlic & Anchovy Sauce

1. Trim broccoli stalks, removing all leaves. Peel and cut the stalks crosswise into ¼-inch slices and separate the tops into florets about ¾ inch in diameter.

2. Bring lightly salted water to a boil in a vegetable steamer. Add the sliced broccoli stalks, cover, and steam 3–5 minutes or until tender. Do not overcook. Set aside. Steam florets for 2–4 minutes and reserve.

3. In a heavy 10-inch skillet, heat the oil over medium-low heat. Add the cayenne pepper, anchovies, and garlic and simmer the mixture, mashing the anchovies with the back of a wooden spoon, until the sauce is thick and smooth. Keep warm.

4. In a large casserole bring lightly salted water to a boil. Add the pasta and cook until just tender. Do not overcook. Immediately add 2 cups cold water to the casserole to stop further cooking. Drain the pasta and return to the casserole.

5. Add the broccoli stalks and florets to the anchovy and garlic sauce and just heat through. Pour the sauce over the pasta; toss gently. Season with salt and pepper and add the Parmesan and optional warm cream. Toss again and serve at once.

1 large bunch fresh broccoli (about 1½ pounds)

Salt

8 tablespoons olive oil, preferably extra-virgin

1 small fresh hot pepper, sliced or diced, crumbled

6–8 flat anchovy fillets

4 large cloves garlic, peeled and finely minced

½ pound pasta shells (ziti or penne)

Freshly ground black pepper

⅓ cup freshly grated Parmesan cheese

⅓ cup warm heavy cream (optional)

SERVES 4–5

Broccoli & Tuna Salad

1–1½ pounds broccoli florets

1 large red bell pepper, seeded, cored, and thinly sliced

1 can (6½ ounces) light tuna, drained and flaked

12 small black oil-cured olives

½ cup thinly sliced red onions

Salt and freshly ground black pepper

2–3 tablespoons red wine vinegar, preferably sherry

1 large clove garlic, peeled and mashed

1 tablespoon finely minced fresh parsley

6 tablespoons olive oil

8 ripe cherry tomatoes, cut in half

GARNISH

6 slices hard salami, cut into thin strips

2 hard-boiled eggs, peeled and quartered

SERVES 4

P·R·E·P·A·R·A·T·I·O·N

1. Bring lightly salted water to a boil in a vegetable steamer. Add the broccoli florets, cover, and steam for 2–4 minutes or until tender. Remove and set aside to cool.

2. In a serving bowl, combine the broccoli florets, red pepper, tuna, olives, and red onions. Season with salt and pepper.

3. Combine 2 tablespoons vinegar with the garlic, parsley, and oil in a food processor or blender and process until smooth. Season with salt and pepper and pour over the broccoli salad. Toss gently and let the salad marinate at room temperature for 1–2 hours.

4. Add the cherry tomatoes to the salad. Taste and correct the seasoning, adding the remaining vinegar if necessary and a large grinding of black pepper. Garnish with the salami and hard-boiled eggs. Chill for 30 minutes before serving.

Pilaf of Rice with Broccoli & Peas

Here is a delicious and colorful rice dish that can be made well ahead of time and reheated. I often double the recipe and keep half the rice for a salad to which I add a well-flavored garlic vinaigrette and finely diced pimientos.

P·R·E·P·A·R·A·T·I·O·N

1. Combine the broth and saffron in a large saucepan. Bring to a boil, reduce heat, and simmer for 25 minutes, tightly covered. Reserve.

2. In another large heavy saucepan melt the butter over medium heat. Add the scallions and cook for 2–3 minutes or until soft but not browned. Add the rice and stock, bring to a boil, reduce heat, cover tightly, and cook for 20 minutes or until the rice is tender.

3. While the rice is cooking prepare *the broccoli:* Bring lightly salted water to a boil in a vegetable steamer, add the florets, cover, and steam until crisp-tender. Reserve.

4. When the rice is done, add the peas, parsley, and broccoli florets. Toss gently with 2 forks so as not to break the florets. Season with salt and pepper. Taste and correct the seasoning, adding the optional butter. Serve hot as an accompaniment to roasts or sautéed meats, poultry, or fish.

3 cups Chicken Stock (page 41) or bouillon
1 teaspoon saffron threads
4 tablespoons unsalted butter
½ cup finely minced scallions
1½ cups long-grain rice
2 cups small broccoli florets
½ pound fresh peas, shelled to yield about ½ cup
3 tablespoons finely minced fresh parsley
Salt and freshly ground white pepper
3 tablespoons unsalted butter for enrichment (optional)

SERVES 4–6

R·E·M·A·R·K·S

If you do not have saffron, you may substitute 1 teaspoon of turmeric. In this case, it is not necessary to steep the turmeric in stock as with saffron. Simply add to the saucepan with rice and stock in Step 2.

Tuscan Broccoli Soup

1 large bunch fresh broccoli (about
  1½ pounds)

3 tablespoons unsalted butter

1 tablespoon olive oil

2 large onions, peeled and finely
  diced

2 large cloves garlic, peeled and
  finely minced

2 medium carrots, peeled and diced

2 stalks celery, finely diced

½ pound smoked pork shoulder
  butt, cut into ½-inch cubes

6–7 cups Beef Stock (page 41) or
  bouillon

¼ cup thin spaghetti, broken into
  ½-inch pieces

Salt and freshly ground black
  pepper

GARNISH

Bowl of freshly grated Parmesan
  cheese

SERVES 6

P·R·E·P·A·R·A·T·I·O·N

1. Trim the broccoli stalks, removing all leaves. Peel and thinly slice the stalks and separate the tops into small even florets.

2. In a heavy 2-quart casserole heat the butter and oil over medium heat. Add the onions, garlic, carrots, celery, and cubed pork butt. Cook the mixture until soft but not browned.

3. Add the stock and broccoli stalks and simmer for 20 minutes or until the stalks are tender.

4. Add the florets and spaghetti, season with salt and a large grinding of black pepper, and simmer until just tender. Taste the soup and correct the seasoning.

5. Serve hot accompanied by a bowl of freshly grated Parmesan cheese.

V·A·R·I·A·T·I·O·N

For a more gutsy soup, I often add 1 cup of cooked white beans and sprinkle each serving with a crumbled blue cheese such as Danish blue or a mild Roquefort.

Sauté of Chicken with Broccoli & Thyme

P·R·E·P·A·R·A·T·I·O·N

1. Dry the chicken pieces thoroughly on paper towels.

2. In a large deep skillet or chicken fryer, heat the oil and butter over medium-high heat. Add the chicken without crowding the pan, partially cover, and sauté until nicely browned on all sides.

3. Season the chicken with salt and pepper and sprinkle with the flour. Cook 2 minutes longer, turning the pieces until evenly coated.

4. Add the wine, bring to a boil, and reduce to 2 tablespoons. Add the garlic, thyme, and ½ cup chicken stock. Cover the pan and cook for 20 minutes.

5. Add the broccoli florets and remaining stock to the pan. Simmer for another 15 minutes or until broccoli is tender.

6. Transfer the chicken and broccoli to a warm serving dish. Discard the garlic from the skillet and whisk in a little of the cornstarch mixture until the sauce lightly coats a spoon. Taste and correct the seasoning.

7. Spoon the sauce over the chicken and broccoli, sprinkle with the parsley, and serve at once.

1 3-pound whole chicken, cut into eighths
3 tablespoons olive oil
1 tablespoon butter
Salt and freshly ground black pepper
1 teaspoon all-purpose flour
⅓ cup dry white wine
3 large cloves garlic, peeled and crushed
3 tablespoons fresh thyme leaves
1 cup Chicken Stock (page 41) or bouillon
3 cups broccoli florets
1 teaspoon cornstarch mixed with a little stock

GARNISH

2 tablespoons finely minced fresh parsley

SERVES 4

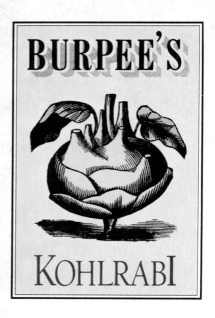

BURPEE'S

KOHLRABI

I am always fascinated by the fact that vegetables are subject to fashion trends, often out for long periods only to be rediscovered by some creative chef. From then on they are to be read about in every food magazine and on restaurant menus. This seems now to be the case with kohlrabi, which may at last be gaining the popularity it deserves. I hope so. The word kohlrabi comes from the German "kohl," meaning cabbage, and "rabi," meaning turnip. The name is appropriate since kohlrabi combines the characteristics of both these vegetables. The edible bulb is like a turnip in shape and flavor, while the leaves resemble those of cabbage and can be used creatively in cooking.

Kohlrabi is extremely popular in Austria, Germany, and all over central and eastern Europe where it is always available tender and sweet. In the United States this vegetable is presently only to be found at specialty greengrocers or in supermarkets in areas that, like some parts of Pennsylvania, are inhabited by people of German descent. Because of the lack of demand, the kohlrabi I sometimes find at the market is past its prime. The bulbs often are large (a sign of stringiness), with limp yellowish greens (a sign of age). As with all vegetables past their prime, old kohlrabi is simply not worth cooking.

Since I grew up eating kohlrabi, sometimes two or three times a week, it has always been an important ingredient in my cooking repertoire. So as soon as I had my own garden I planted this vegetable, discovering that it is easy to grow, extremely productive, and very quick to mature.

Young kohlrabi is delicious finely sliced and served as part of a crudité platter along with a tangy dip. It can be steamed, sautéed, braised, pureed, or pickled. In fact, kohlrabi can be substituted in every recipe calling for turnips. I often add a handful of cubed kohlrabi to the pan juices of a roasting chicken. By the time the chicken is done, so is the vegetable, adding a sweet taste to the sauce and absorbing the flavorful juices of the chicken. Because of its natural sweetness and lovely pale color, kohlrabi works beautifully when combined with carrots and peas in a

spring fricassee (see page 53) or used in a creamy soup spiked with fresh leeks (page 55).

To prepare kohlrabi you may peel it before cooking, removing all the leaves and skin, or cook it and then peel when the vegetable is tender. The very young bulbs can be sliced and braised in a deep skillet with a little butter, broth, and seasoning. Older bulbs are best reserved for purees, possibly in combination with potatoes or carrots.

S·T·O·R·A·G·E

Remove all the foliage from the bulbs and store bulbs in perforated plastic bags for up to a week. Store the leaves, which can keep for two to three days, in separate plastic bags. Kohlrabi leaves can be steamed or braised and then finished with a touch of butter, cream or sour cream, and a sprinkling of herbs.

G·A·R·D·E·N·I·N·G

I enjoy kohlrabi so much that I sometimes make several successive plantings in spring and again starting in midsummer. The bulbs, which grow just above ground, are ready for harvest in seven to eight weeks. Very early (45 to 50 days) is Grand Duke Hybrid, a light-skinned variety with crisp white flesh. Early Purple Vienna, with purplish skin and very pale green flesh, matures about ten days later. Kohlrabi's soil must be kept constantly moist, so it is best to apply a thick mulch around the plants. The mulch will also smother weeds, important because the shallow roots of kohlrabi are easily damaged during weeding.

H·A·R·V·E·S·T·I·N·G

The perfect time to harvest kohlrabi is when bulbs are barely two inches across. Any wider than three inches and bulbs quickly become tough. Use a sharp knife to cut stems near ground level, about an inch below the bulbs.

KOHLRABI PICKLES

Trim, peel and cut 1 pound kohlrabi into ¼-inch-wide strips. Place in colander, sprinkle with ¼ cup coarse salt and drain 2 hours. Rinse off salt, place in towel and squeeze out excess liquid. Place in bowl and set aside. Combine 1 cup white distilled vinegar and ½ cup sugar in saucepan. Bring to a boil and pour over kohlrabi. Cool and divide between two 1-pint jars and "pack."

Butter-Braised Kohlrabi with Brown Sugar

P · R · E · P · A · R · A · T · I · O · N

1. In a medium skillet, melt the butter over medium heat. Add the kohlrabi slices and toss to coat evenly with the butter. Season with salt and pepper. Add the water, cover, and simmer until tender, about 10–12 minutes. If all the water evaporates during cooking, add a bit more. If any liquid remains in the skillet after cooking, remove the cover and cook until evaporated.

2. Add the brown sugar and toss gently until the sugar melts and the kohlrabi slices are nicely caramelized. Serve hot.

3 tablespoons unsalted butter
6 medium kohlrabi (about 1½ pounds), peeled and thinly sliced
Salt and freshly ground white pepper
⅓ cup water
2 tablespoons dark brown sugar

SERVES 4–5

R · E · M · A · R · K · S

You may give the dish a sweet-and-sour taste by adding 1–2 tablespoons red wine vinegar when adding the brown sugar.

Casserole-Roasted Chicken with Kohlrabi, Carrots & Thyme

1 whole chicken (about 3–3½
  pounds), trussed
Salt and freshly ground black
  pepper
3 tablespoons fresh thyme
2 tablespoons unsalted butter
1 teaspoon corn oil
3 small onions, peeled and cut in
  half through root end
1¼ cups Chicken Stock (page 41)
  or bouillon
4 small kohlrabi, peeled and
  quartered
3 medium carrots, trimmed, peeled,
  and cut crosswise into ½-inch
  pieces
3 large cloves garlic, peeled and
  crushed
1 recipe Beurre Manié (page 20)

GARNISH

Sprigs of fresh parsley

SERVES 4

After the chicken has been "casserole roasted" you may quarter it and run it under the broiler to brown and crisp the skin. In this case serve the sauce on the side.

P·R·E·P·A·R·A·T·I·O·N

1. Preheat the oven to 350°. Season the chicken with salt, pepper, and thyme.

2. In a large heavy skillet, heat the butter and oil. When very hot, add the chicken and brown on all sides. Transfer to an oval casserole and set aside.

3. Discard all but 2 tablespoons of fat from the skillet, add the onions, cut side down, and sauté until lightly browned. Add ¾ cup stock, bring to a boil, and transfer onions and stock to the casserole.

4. Add the kohlrabi, carrots, and garlic to the casserole. Bring slowly to a boil on top of the stove, cover tightly, and place in the center of the preheated oven. Braise the chicken for 1 hour to 1 hour 10 minutes, turning it once or twice during cooking time and basting it with the pan juices. The chicken is done when the juices run pale yellow. Transfer it to a baking dish and set aside. Remove the vegetables with a slotted spoon to a side dish, cover, and reserve.

5. Carefully degrease the pan juices, adding the remaining stock to the casserole. Bring to a boil on top of the stove and reduce by ⅓. Whisk in bits of beurre manié until the sauce lightly coats a spoon. Taste and correct the seasoning. Add the vegetables to the sauce and keep warm.

6. Remove and discard the trussing string from the chicken, quarter, and place on a serving platter. Spoon the vegetables around the chicken and the sauce over. Garnish with sprigs of parsley and serve accompanied by rice pilaf.

Fricassee of Kohlrabi, Peas & Carrots in Mint Butter

1. Bring plenty of lightly salted water to a boil in a large saucepan. Add the kohlrabi and cook 5–6 minutes or until just tender. Drain and reserve.

2. Bring more water to a boil. Add the carrots and cook until just tender. Drain and reserve.

3. Place peas in a saucepan with water to cover. Add ½ teaspoon sugar and pinch of salt. Bring to a boil, reduce heat, and simmer until just tender. Drain and reserve.

4. In a large skillet, melt the butter over medium heat. Add the vegetables and cook for 3–4 minutes without browning. Add the sour cream and mint. Toss gently and correct the seasoning. Serve hot as an accompaniment to chicken or veal preparations.

6–8 small kohlrabi, trimmed, peeled, and cut into ¾-inch cubes
Salt
3 medium carrots, peeled and cut into ½-inch dice
1 pound fresh peas or 1 cup shelled
½ teaspoon granulated sugar
4 tablespoons unsalted butter
2 tablespoons sour cream
2 tablespoons finely minced fresh mint
Freshly ground white pepper

SERVES 4–5

Viennese Kohlrabi

6 medium kohlrabi (about 1½ pounds), trimmed, peeled, and cut into ¼-inch-wide matchsticks

Salt

¾ cup sour cream

1 teaspoon paprika, preferably imported

1 teaspoon all-purpose flour

4 tablespoons unsalted butter

4 tablespoons finely minced scallions

¼ cup Chicken Stock (page 41) or bouillon

Freshly ground white pepper

SERVES 4–5

P·R·E·P·A·R·A·T·I·O·N

1. Bring lightly salted water to a boil in a vegetable steamer. Add the kohlrabi, cover, and steam for 3–4 minutes or until just tender. Remove and set aside.

2. In a small bowl, combine the sour cream, paprika, and flour. Mix until well blended and reserve.

3. Melt the butter in a heavy 10-inch skillet. Add the scallions and cook over medium heat for 1 minute. Add the kohlrabi and toss with the butter and scallions. Add the chicken stock, raise the heat, and cook until the stock has reduced to a glaze.

4. Reduce heat, stir in the sour cream mixture, and cook for 2 minutes longer. Season with salt and pepper and serve at once.

Cream of Kohlrabi & Potato Soup

P·R·E·P·A·R·A·T·I·O·N

1. In a large casserole, melt the butter over medium heat. Add the onion and potatoes and cook until the onion is soft but not browned.

2. Rinse the sliced leeks under cold water, drain, and add to the casserole together with the diced kohlrabi. Season with salt and pepper. Add the stock, bring to a boil, reduce heat, and simmer partially covered until the vegetables are very soft, about 35 minutes.

3. Cool the soup and puree in a food processor or blender until smooth. Return the soup to the casserole. Add the crème fraîche or heavy cream/sour cream mixture, and correct the seasoning.

4. Serve hot, garnished with minced chives and accompanied by a crusty loaf of French bread.

3 tablespoons unsalted butter

1 large onion, peeled and finely diced

2 medium all-purpose potatoes, peeled and diced

2 small leeks, trimmed of all but 2 inches of greens and finely sliced

4 medium kohlrabi (about 1 pound untrimmed), peeled and diced

Salt and freshly ground white pepper

6 cups Chicken Stock (page 41) or bouillon

1 cup Crème Fraîche (below) or ½ cup heavy cream plus ¼ cup sour cream

GARNISH

2 tablespoons finely minced fresh chives

SERVES 5–6

CRÈME FRAÎCHE

For homemade crème fraîche combine 2 cups heavy cream (not ultrapasteurized) and 6 tablespoons buttermilk in glass jar. Whisk until combined and set aside at room temperature for 24 hours. Chill until ready to use.

BURPEE'S

SALAD GREENS & OTHER GREENS

Over the past few years growing greens has become an exciting part of the home gardening experience. Aside from the classics, such as romaine, Boston, and other head lettuce, you will occasionally find lovely leaf lettuce, dandelion greens, tiny hearts of Bibb lettuce, and endives. This is not to mention the new "in" greens, such as radicchio, and the latest fad, corn salad, or what the French call *mâche*. For the home gardener this great variety is equally inspiring.

Essentially, all greens can be categorized as being either buttery (mild tasting) or acidic (having stronger, more assertive flavors). Today's cooks should be familiar with the character of the various greens, including those that double as cooked vegetables, such as collards, dandelion, sorrel, and mustard.

The new American cuisine is rediscovering and refining the salad, and doing so with style, innovation, and great creativity. Indeed, salads have taken center stage, and while some of the theatrical touches may be overplayed and somewhat contrived, one thing has become quite clear: Cooks, restaurant chefs, and gardeners care very much about their salad greens. In addition to experimenting with a variety of lettuces, they are creating exciting dressings using unusual oils and vinegars, mustards, and herbs to achieve the kind of harmony that can set a salad apart and make it a focal point of a meal.

It is fun to add an unusual leaf or two to your salad bowl, but a good green salad really depends on three basic ingredients only: the freshest greens, the best oil, and the best vinegar. What is absolutely essential is knowing both the proportion of oil to vinegar for a well-balanced vinaigrette and the amount of dressing to use with regard to the quantity of greens.

ICEBERG (HEAD) LETTUCE

Needless to say, iceberg fresh from the garden is better and crisper from that uninspiring ball you find wrapped in cellophane in most supermarkets and certainly excellent in sandwiches and in combination with tomatoes, cucumbers, and radishes in a Greek

salad. Otherwise, iceberg lacks the kind of flexibility a leafy vegetable should have in a salad bowl.

ROMAINE LETTUCE

Romaine is considered an all-purpose lettuce in Mediterranean Europe, where it is often the only choice. In America good romaine is available year-round in supermarkets and grocery stores, but when it is garden-fresh, it is a different lettuce. Milder and more tender, the fresh leaves have an affinity to just about every other green, cooked or uncooked. In Spain, where romaine is king, the tender leaves are usually served as an appetizer together with a finely sliced spicy hard sausage, some oil-cured black olives, a few radishes, and crusty bread. Cruets of olive oil and vinegar are always on hand and everyone seasons his own salad to taste.

BOSTON LETTUCE

Boston is to central and northern Europe what romaine is to the south. It is the everyday lettuce that most cooks pick up at the market and it is served in every restaurant. In France hearts of Boston are classically cooked together with young fresh peas and some tiny spring onions. Whoever first thought of this marriage did, indeed, create one made in heaven.

When the heads are tight, crisp, and firm, this is an excellent lettuce that allows for creativity as long as the added greens are light-textured and have an interesting bite. Boston lettuce is a fragile green and should be tossed with the dressing of your choice—but without adding salt—at the very last minute to ensure crispness.

BIBB LETTUCE

Bibb lettuce is considered the most refined of the buttery lettuces. It has a texture similar to Boston, but the smaller, tighter heads and crisper leaves are more flavorful and hold up better in a dressing. Since store-bought Bibb is the most expensive of all lettuces, it is worthwhile to grow a good amount of this lovely salad green in the garden. Bibb is a wonderful addition to a *mesclun,* the French term for a mixed salad of three to four greens, since it holds its shape so gracefully and lends its buttery yet assertive taste to the other greens without overwhelming them.

LOOSE-LEAF LETTUCE
(RED AND GREEN LEAF)

Loose-leaf lettuce is extremely easy to grow, accounting for its popularity in the spring garden. Hot and the plants do well even in poor soil. They mature quickly, producing attractive large leaves that are both tender and mild. Of all lettuces, loose-leaf has become the star of the new American salad phenomenon, mainly because it makes an excellent bed to composed salads but also because its mild texture leaves room for many innovative touches. I like to use a tossed salad of loose-leaf lettuce as a backdrop to a julienne of mesquite-grilled chicken breasts (page 71) or as an accompaniment to creamy corn custards (page 76). Tossed with the proper amount of cool mustardy vinaigrette, loose-leaf is simply delicious by itself. With the addition of a few dandelion greens, the heart of a tiny Bibb lettuce, and possibly the "in" touch of a few bright red radicchio leaves, you have the makings of a memorable salad.

These are some of my favorite combinations of lettuces for salads: spinach, red leaf lettuce and Belgian endive (also nice with sliced red onion and sliced raw mushrooms added); romaine, sliced radishes, scallions and arugula; corn salad, oakleaf lettuce, dandelion greens and young sorrel.

G · A · R · D · E · N · I · N · G

Cool-loving lettuces need full sun when sown in early spring or autumn, while summer crops flourish only if shaded during midday. Adequate shade can be provided by interplanting lettuce among taller plants such as broccoli, or by sowing rows of lettuce next to rows of corn or trellis-grown beans. It is essential that soil remain moist and relatively cool, especially when heads are just beginning to develop. This is most easily accomplished by surrounding the seedlings with a two- to four-inch-thick mulch of salt hay or grass clippings.

Whenever possible, wait until plants reach the "baby" stage before thinning, at which point lettuce makes wonderful eating. For a long harvest season in a small space, thin plants gradually, pulling and using every other plant each time you need some for a salad. When you're down to the suggested spacing (four to twelve inches apart), pick just the outer leaves from each plant and leave the inner ones to mature. Finally, near the end of the season, pull the entire plant.

If this sounds too complicated, and if you have a bit more garden space, plant lettuce seeds every ten to fourteen days until midspring, allowing enough time for the last sowing to mature before hot weather starts.

Wash and refrigerate fresh-picked lettuce immediately to prevent leaves from wilting.

DANDELIONS

When I was a child, picking dandelion greens in spring was an unbroken tradition. In mid- or late March my father and I would set out to the fields on Saturday mornings looking for the young tender dandelions and pop them into a basket. By lunchtime we would return and present my mother with these tangy young wild greens, which soon became the center part of the meal, usually accompanied by the local garlic-studded sausage, cooked on the grill, and a crusty loaf of farmer's bread.

Dandelions that are really young and tender are still a rare find at the market. Growing your own is very rewarding since you can pick the leaves at the right stage, leaving the more mature ones for a quick stir-fry to be added to a pasta dish. In France, where dandelion is called *pissenlit,* it is served in a classic preparation that is fast becoming stylish in this country as well. Diced smoky bacon is cooked in a skillet and the fat is tossed with the greens. A splash of vinegar and seasoning is all that is needed to complete this flavorful salad. If you are more adventurous you can also make the salad with duck cracklings, using some rendered duck fat. One of the simplest and most satisfying ways to serve a dandelion salad is with the sweet-and-sour Pennsylvania Dutch dressing on page 75.

Mature dandelions can be used for a simple stir-fry with two to three sliced cloves of garlic and some minced jalapeño pepper. Tossed with some freshly cooked pasta and seasoned with freshly ground black pepper, it makes a delicious and quick-to-prepare appetizer.

S·T·O·R·A·G·E

When buying dandelions, look for small crisp leaves that have the mildest flavor.

To store, place bunches in plastic bags in the vegetable bin of the refrigerator. Do not wash until just before using. If dandelions are picked with their roots still attached, wrap the roots in damp paper towels and then place in plastic bags.

G·A·R·D·E·N·I·N·G

Dandelion seeds available to vegetable gardeners produce plants as resilient as those that pop up across lawns each spring. But cultivated dandelion boasts leaves that are larger, thicker, and tastier than those from the wild plant. Blanching will help keep the leaves tender enough to eat raw. Simply tie the foliage together so that the outer leaves prevent light from penetrating to the inner leaves.

Be sure to dig out and discard any remaining dandelion plants before they flower and go to seed; otherwise, dandelion will be your primary crop next year.

ARUGULA

It's called *roquette* in France, rocket or rocket salad in England, and *rucola* in Italy. American horticulturists recognize it as rugula, but somehow most American cooks have settled on arugula, which I've seen spelled a dozen ways. The botanical name is *Eruca sativa*.

SESAME VINAIGRETTE

Here is a somewhat unusual vinaigrette that makes for a nice change of pace:

In a jar combine 1 clove garlic, peeled and mashed, with 1 tablespoon Dijon mustard, 1/4 teaspoon dry mustard, 1 tablespoon thin soy sauce, 2 tablespoons red wine vinegar, 8 tablespoons peanut oil and 2 tablespoons sesame oil.

Cover jar and shake dressing until well blended. Season with salt and pepper. Just before serving, add 1/2 cup minced scallions. Serve slightly chilled over tossed greens or as a light sauce with grilled fish or shellfish. The dressing can be stored in the refrigerator for 4 to 5 days.

Variation:
Place the dressing in the food processor and add 1/4 cup cilantro leaves and blend the mixture until smooth.

Many gardeners and cooks consider arugula an Italian salad green. Although it is grown in France and Greece, it is by far more popular in Italy than in any other European country. In recent years this interesting peppery green has become the "in" green in this country, where it is often combined with tiny radicchio leaves, a milder leafy lettuce, or finely julienned Belgian endives and then lightly tossed in extra-virgin olive oil and a touch of red wine vinegar.

To those of us who live in areas that cater to Italian cooks, arugula is a familiar sight at most local vegetable stores. Arugula salads are commonly offered at Italian restaurants, usually in combination with other milder greens that offset the rather sharp taste of this distinctive green.

Unfortunately, store-bought arugula is often too mature and lacking in freshness, which renders it overly strong and pungent. Growing your own arugula is one of the great joys of vegetable gardening—a springtime treasure. Since it is a fast-growing green, you can pick arugula at the peak of flavor, when leaves are about two to three inches high.

S·T·O·R·A·G·E

Arugula keeps well for as long as a week in a plastic bag in the vegetable drawer of the refrigerator.

G·A·R·D·E·N·I·N·G

As with so many greens, the first arugula crop should be sown very early in spring so it can benefit from the season's cool and moist conditions to the fullest. Plants are ready to harvest in about five weeks. Grow successive crops during spring and begin sowing again in late summer for harvests during fall. Like dandelion, arugula is a rampant weed if it goes to seed, so pull plants before the hot weather causes them to bolt.

Other Greens

In the last few years some of the most traditional greens have emerged as the leafy stars of the French nouvelle cuisine and the new American cuisine.

Sorrel, a hardy perennial that had been relegated to a corner of the vegetable garden, was suddenly rediscovered and is now used with great creativity in many dishes. Other greens, mustard and collard in particular, which never seemed to shine beyond their regional boundaries, are finding their way into many vegetable gardens, supermarkets, and specialty stores and are being picked up by both gardeners and cooks with great enthusiasm.

Although these greens have been around for years, they well deserve their new stardom. Not only are they easy to grow, but they are often interchangeable in many preparations and add flavor, texture, and color to many soups, stews, and salads.

COLLARDS

For years collards were considered a Southern green, one that was associated primarily with soul food. But in recent years, with the new vogue of regional cooking sweeping the country, cooks and restaurant chefs have discovered collards, using them with creativity and imagination.

Closely related to kale, collards have large and somewhat coarse pale green leaves that, when cooked, have an interesting taste. Most Southern states raise large quantities of both collard and mustard greens, and the regional way of cooking these greens has been a rather lengthy braising with some smoked pork butt or a ham bone. Although collards take well to the smokiness of bacon, I see no reason to overcook this good-natured green. Rather, I find that young collards can be quickly stir-fried in good olive oil with some sliced garlic, make a fine addition to spring and summer soups, and are delicious when combined in a well-flavored custard (see page 82).

S·T·O·R·A·G·E

Although they can be stored in the coldest part of the refrigerator for a day or two, collards should be cooked as soon as possible since they tend to wilt quickly.

G·A·R·D·E·N·I·N·G

It may come as a surprise that this Southern favorite tolerates cold in the garden better than does cabbage, another collard relative. Unlike many other members of the cabbage family, collards also tolerate heat. Because a single plant can be harvested throughout the season, successive plantings are unnecessary. For summer and autumn picking, I sow seeds in very early spring, as soon as the soil can be worked easily. If you garden in the South, make a second sowing in late summer for harvests during fall and winter. To avoid diseases, do not plant collards in the same spots where cole crops grew the previous year. But do give the plants plenty of room. Collards, which are also known as tree cabbage due to their size and shape, may eventually become three feet high and wide. For smaller, more compact plants, try a variety named Vates.

H·A·R·V·E·S·T·I·N·G

Pick the outermost leaves before they become tough. The central rosette of young foliage also makes good eating, but plucking it out puts an end to the plant's productivity. Leaves harvested after a light autumn frost tend to be particularly flavorful.

MUSTARD GREENS

In the United States mustard greens are extremely popular in the South, where they are cooked in a similar fashion to collard greens, usually with a piece of ham bone or salt pork. But with the growing demand around the country for interesting regional greens, you can now find mustard greens featured on the menus of some of the most innovative restaurants.

Although more and more markets offer mustard greens, to-day's gardener has a choice of several fast-growing varieties, any of which makes a wonderful addition to the spring garden. None is better than Fordhook Fancy, whose pretty foliage offers delightfully mild flavor.

S·T·O·R·A·G·E

Store unwashed leaves in a plastic bag. The fresh greens will keep up to five days. Garden-picked mustard greens have to be rinsed in several changes of warm water before drying in a salad spinner or a kitchen towel.

G·A·R·D·E·N·I·N·G

Although modern mustard green varieties are relatively slow to bolt, the plants require cool temperatures for best results. Start sowing seeds as soon as soil can be worked in spring, and be sure to fertilize before planting. Only in fertile soil kept evenly moist will mustard plants grow rapidly enough to be ready before the weather warms in mid- to late spring. For fall harvests, I like to make a second sowing in late summer.

H·A·R·V·E·S·T·I·N·G

Like all greens, mustard is at its best when picked at a young, tender stage—about a month after planting.

SORREL

Ten years ago sorrel was practically an unknown green in this country. Even in France and England, where it is grown as a perennial in many gardens, it was considered a "vintage" green, only to be used occasionally in soup. But when the Troisgros brothers, two extraordinarily gifted chefs from the Lyons area,

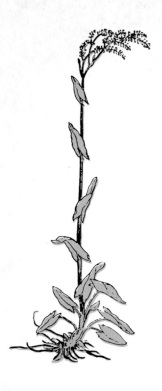

created a sublime dish of sautéed salmon cutlet in a creamy sorrel sauce, this forgotten green became a star overnight. Now there is scarcely a fine restaurant in Europe or the United States that does not use sorrel in one way or another.

Sorrel, which grows wild in Russia and Scandinavia, is used primarily for two classic soups. The Russian version uses potatoes, while the French *potage à l'oseille* is a velvety soup using an enrichment of egg yolks, cream, and a touch of lemon.

The puckery taste of sorrel has led to its being named "sourgrass," and it is its somewhat sour flavor that makes this green so interesting. Although very young sorrel leaves can be used sparingly in salads, the green is at its best when melted down like spinach—with only the water that clings to the leaves—and then pureed. In combination with cream, it is the best accompaniment to salmon cutlets, scallops, or fillets of sole. A fine julienne of three to four tablespoons of raw sorrel leaves is often all that is needed to perk up a cream sauce or soup.

Since sorrel is a perennial that comes up year after year with little care, every gardener can enjoy this superb "vintage" green; every gardening cook will wonder how he or she got along without it.

S · T · O · R · A · G · E

Store sorrel leaves in a plastic bag in the refrigerator and use within a day or two of buying or picking. Sorrel has to be washed in several changes of lukewarm water and cooked with just the water that clings to its leaves.

G · A · R · D · E · N · I · N · G

Unlike free-spreading wild sorrel, clump-forming cultivated sorrel is reasonably easy to keep under control. Choose a permanent spot for the plants where soil is rich and moderately acid and sunlight is direct for at least a few hours daily. Established plants should be fertilized each spring and watered generously throughout the growing season. In midseason I take the time to cut off any developing seed stalks. Otherwise, sorrel would propagate itself like a weed. I also pick off old or yellow leaves to encourage plants to continue producing desirable fresh foliage. Every few years tired clumps should be rejuvenated. Simply dig up the plants, divide them, and then replant the healthiest divisions.

H · A · R · V · E · S · T · I · N · G

Always pick the outer leaves first, leaving a rosette of foliage within to ensure additional harvests later on. It is a good idea to cut some foliage regularly even if it is not needed for the kitchen. Otherwise, plants may lose their vigor and outer leaves their tenderness.

R · E · C · I · P · E · S

Mixed Salad Greens with Fried Bread & Mozzarella

1. Combine the lettuces in a large mixing bowl, cover, and chill until serving time.

2. Preheat the broiler.

3. Rub each side of the bread slices with the cut clove of garlic.

4. Heat the oil in a heavy 10-inch skillet over medium heat. Add the bread and sauté until nicely browned on both sides. Regulate the heat so as not to burn the bread. Transfer to a double layer of paper towels.

5. Spread one side of each sautéed bread slice with a bit of anchovy paste or minced anchovy fillets. Top each with a slice of mozzarella and place on a baking sheet. Set in the broiler 6 inches from the source of heat and broil until the cheese is just heated through and begins to melt. Remove and reserve.

6. Toss the greens with the vinaigrette and place on each of 6 individual dinner plates. Set one fried bread in the center of each plate, sprinkle with a few capers, and serve at once.

R·E·M·A·R·K·S

As long as the greens are not tossed with the vinaigrette, they can be washed and chilled well ahead of serving. The bread can be fried and assembled in advance but must be broiled just before serving.

8 cups loosely packed mixed salad lettuces, including corn salad and small leaves of radicchio, washed and dried

6 slices French bread, about ½-inch thick

1 large clove garlic, peeled and cut in half

3 tablespoons olive oil, preferably extra-virgin

2 teaspoons anchovy paste or 4 flat anchovy fillets, finely minced

6 slices whole milk mozzarella, ¼-inch thick (about ¼ pound)

4–6 tablespoons Garlic Vinaigrette (below)

GARNISH

2 teaspoons tiny capers, drained

SERVES 6

GARLIC VINAIGRETTE

In a small jar, combine 6 tablespoons extra-virgin olive oil, 1½ tablespoons sherry vinegar, 1 large clove garlic, peeled and mashed. Shake until well blended. Season with salt and freshly ground pepper, then chill. Bring back to room temperature about 30 minutes before serving.

2 whole chicken breasts, boned,
   skinned, and cut into 1-inch
   cubes

THE MARINADE

1 tablespoon finely minced fresh
   gingerroot

2 large cloves garlic, peeled and
   finely minced

1 teaspoon cumin seeds, roasted
   and crushed

½ teaspoon coriander seeds,
   roasted and crushed

½ teaspoon ground cardamom

⅓ cup yogurt

3 tablespoons olive oil

3 tablespoons freshly squeezed
   lemon juice

1 small fresh hot pepper, minced,
   or dried, crumbled

THE DRESSING

1 medium clove garlic, peeled and
   finely minced

½ teaspoon ground cumin

1 teaspoon Dijon mustard

1 tablespoon red wine vinegar

6 tablespoons olive oil

2 tablespoons yogurt or sour cream

Coarse salt and freshly ground
   black pepper

THE SALAD

3 tablespoons thinly sliced red
   onion

6 cups mixed greens (about 6
   ounces total), leaves separated,
   washed, and dried on paper
   towels

3 small Belgian endives, cored and
   quartered lengthwise

6 radishes, thinly sliced

GARNISH

Ripe cherry tomatoes, quartered

SERVES 4

Grilled Indian Chicken on a Bed of Greens with Yogurt & Garlic Dressing

1. Start by marinating *the chicken:* Place the chicken cubes in a shallow dish and set aside.

2. Combine all the ingredients for the marinade in a small bowl. Whisk until well blended and pour over the cubed chicken. Marinate at room temperature for 1 hour.

3. While the chicken is marinating, prepare *the dressing:* Combine the garlic, cumin, mustard, vinegar, olive oil, and yogurt in a small covered jar. Cover tightly and shake until the dressing becomes thick and creamy. Season with salt and pepper to taste.

4. Place the dressing in the bottom of a large salad bowl. Top with the red onion, mixed greens, endives, and radishes. Do not toss. Cover and chill until serving time.

5. Prepare the charcoal grill.

6. Remove the chicken from the marinade and thread on 4 skewers. Sprinkle with coarse salt and pepper and place on grill over hot coals. Grill about 2 minutes per side or until just done. Do not overcook. Reserve.

7. To serve, toss the salad and divide among 4 individual dinner plates. Top each salad with grilled chicken cubes and garnish with cherry tomatoes. Serve at once.

Warm Goat Cheese Salad

3 tablespoons olive oil

6 slices French bread, cut ½-inch thick

2 small cloves garlic, peeled and cut in half

2 tablespoons red wine vinegar, preferably sherry

6–8 tablespoons walnut oil

Salt and freshly ground black pepper

½ cup finely diced prosciutto or smoked ham

½ small red onion, peeled and thinly sliced

2 small bunches of arugula and/or 2 cups corn salad leaves, trimmed, washed, and dried

2 small heads Bibb lettuce, leaves separated, washed, and dried

1 small head radicchio, leaves separated

2 Belgian endives, trimmed, cored, and quartered lengthwise

6 slices of young goat cheese, preferably Montrachet, Chabichou, or Crottin, cut ½-inch thick

12 walnut halves

4–6 fresh shiitake mushrooms, quartered and sautéed in olive oil (optional)

SERVES 6

P·R·E·P·A·R·A·T·I·O·N

1. In a large nonstick skillet heat the olive oil over medium heat. Add the bread slices and sauté on both sides until lightly browned. Remove from the skillet and rub with the cut cloves of garlic and set aside.

2. In the bottom of a large salad bowl, combine the vinegar and walnut oil. Whisk the dressing until well blended, season with salt and pepper, and add the diced prosciutto or smoked ham and sliced onion. Top with the arugula and/or corn salad, Bibb, radicchio, and endives. Do not toss. Cover and chill until serving.

3. Just before serving, preheat the broiler.

4. Place a slice of goat cheese on each sautéed bread slice. Run under the broiler until the cheese begins to melt. Immediately remove from the broiler and set aside.

5. Toss the salad and correct the seasoning. Add the walnuts. Place the salad on individual salad plates and top each with a melted cheese toast. Garnish with the optional sautéed warm shiitake mushrooms and serve immediately.

Spicy Shrimp Salad with Two Lettuces

1. In a large saucepan bring lightly salted water to a boil. Add the shrimp and bring the water back to a boil. Immediately remove from the heat and let the shrimp cool in the poaching liquid. Peel and cube. Transfer to a large mixing bowl.

2. Add the red pepper, parsley, scallions, sliced chili pepper, and lemon slices to the shrimp. Set aside.

3. In a small bowl combine the lime juice, vinegar, and olive oil. Season with salt, pepper, and cayenne to taste. Add the crushed garlic and oregano and whisk the mixture until well blended. Pour the dressing over the shrimp and vegetables and toss lightly. Chill for 4–6 hours or overnight.

4. Just before serving, remove and discard the garlic and lemon slices. Taste and correct the seasoning. If the salad is too spicy, add the optional sliced avocado. Serve slightly chilled on individual plates lined with leaves of Boston lettuce and radicchio tossed with a little garlic vinaigrette.

1 pound small shrimp

Salt

1 red bell pepper, seeded and thinly sliced

¾ cup finely minced fresh parsley

½ cup finely minced scallions (about 3 medium)

1 fresh hot green chili pepper, thinly sliced, or dried, crumbled

1 small lemon, unpeeled and thinly sliced

Juice of 2 limes

3 tablespoons red wine vinegar

½ cup olive oil, preferably extra-virgin

Freshly ground black pepper

⅛ teaspoon cayenne pepper

3 large cloves garlic, peeled and crushed

2 tablespoons fresh oregano leaves

1 ripe avocado, peeled and sliced (optional)

Leaves of Boston lettuce and radicchio

Garlic Vinaigrette (page 69)

SERVES 6–8

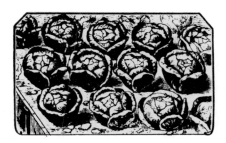

Spicy Fried Chicken Wings with Mixed Greens in Oriental Dressing

P·R·E·P·A·R·A·T·I·O·N

THE CHICKEN WINGS

8 chicken wings, tips removed and discarded or reserved for stock
⅛ teaspoon cayenne pepper
1 teaspoon dried thyme
1 teaspoon cumin seeds, roasted and crushed
1 teaspoon coarse salt
Freshly ground black pepper
Flour for dredging
Peanut oil for frying

THE VINAIGRETTE

5 tablespoons peanut oil
1 tablespoon thin soy sauce
1 tablespoon red wine vinegar
2 teaspoons granulated sugar
½ teaspoon dry mustard
1 medium clove garlic, peeled and mashed
2 medium scallions, finely minced
Salt and freshly ground black pepper

THE SALAD

12 snow peas, strings removed
1 cup mung bean sprouts
2 pickling cucumbers, peeled, seeded, and cut into thin matchsticks

1. Start by marinating the *chicken wings:* Cut each wing in half at the joint. Place the pieces in a large stainless steel bowl and sprinkle with the cayenne, thyme, cumin, coarse salt, and black pepper. Toss to coat well with the spices and let sit at room temperature for 1 hour.

2. While the chicken wings are marinating, prepare the *vinaigrette and salad:* In a large mixing bowl combine the peanut oil, soy sauce, vinegar, sugar, mustard, and garlic. Whisk until well blended. Add the scallions and season carefully with salt and pepper. Set bowl aside.

3. Bring lightly salted water to a boil in a vegetable steamer, add the snow peas, cover, and steam for 1 minute. Drain and cut into a thin julienne.

4. Add the snow peas, bean sprouts, cucumbers, and lettuce to the bowl containing the vinaigrette, in that order. Do not toss. Cover and refrigerate until serving time.

5. Fry the *chicken wings:* Dredge the wings lightly in flour, shaking off the excess.

6. In a large heavy skillet or chicken fryer, heat peanut oil to the depth of ½ inch over medium-high heat. When hot, add the chicken wings and cook for 10–12 minutes until crisp and nicely browned on all sides. Regulate the heat so as not to burn the wings. Remove from the skillet with kitchen tongs and place on paper towels to drain.

7. Heat 1 tablespoon peanut oil in a small skillet over medium-high heat, add the shiitake mushrooms, and toss in the hot oil for 30 seconds. Add the warm mushrooms to the cool salad and toss with the vinaigrette.

8. To serve, divide the salad among 4 individual dinner plates. Top each portion with 4 pieces of fried chicken and serve immediately with a crusty loaf of French bread.

4 cups mixed salad greens
1 tablespoon peanut oil
4 fresh shiitake mushrooms, stemmed and thinly sliced

SERVES 4

Dandelions with Pennsylvania Dutch Warm Dressing

P·R·E·P·A·R·A·T·I·O·N

1. Place the dandelions in a large mixing bowl and set aside.

2. In a small skillet, cook the bacon over low heat, until just crisp. Remove with a slotted spoon to a side dish and reserve.

3. Combine the egg yolks, vinegar, sugar, and mustard in a small saucepan. Whisk until well blended. Place over low heat and whisk constantly until the dressing becomes thick and smooth. Be careful not to overcook or the egg yolks will curdle.

4. Immediately transfer to a small mixing bowl. Add the chives and season with salt and a large grinding of black pepper.

5. Pour the warm dressing over the greens and toss gently until the leaves are well coated. Place the salad on individual serving plates and sprinkle each with some of the bacon. Serve at once.

½ pound young dandelion greens (about 8 cups), stemmed, washed, and dried on paper towels
6 ounces sliced smoked bacon, cut into ¼-inch pieces
4 egg yolks
6 tablespoons white wine vinegar
1 tablespoon granulated sugar
Pinch of dry mustard
3 tablespoons finely minced fresh chives
Salt and freshly ground black pepper

SERVES 4–6

Greens with Warm Corn Custards & Honey-Cumin Vinaigrette

THE SALAD

2 tablespoons red wine vinegar

6–8 tablespoons olive oil

2 teaspoons pure honey

½ teaspoon ground cumin

Salt and freshly ground black pepper

2 cups each: young spinach leaves, corn salad, arugula, and red leaf lettuce, stemmed, washed, and dried on paper towels (about 6 ounces total)

Leaves of 1 small radicchio (optional)

THE CORN CUSTARDS

Butter

3 large whole eggs

1½ cups heavy cream

1 cup cooked corn kernels

1 tablespoon finely minced red onion

1–2 tablespoons finely minced green chili pepper

Salt and freshly ground white pepper

GARNISH

4 thick slices smoked bacon, cooked until medium crisp, crumbled

SERVES 4–6

P·R·E·P·A·R·A·T·I·O·N

1. Start by making *the salad:* In a large mixing bowl, combine the vinegar, oil, honey, and cumin. Whisk until well blended and season with salt and pepper. Top with the spinach, corn salad, arugula, red leaf lettuce, and optional radicchio. Do not toss. Cover the salad and refrigerate until needed.

2. Preheat oven to 350°.

3. *The corn custards:* Generously butter 4 to 6 individual 4-ounce porcelain ramequins and set aside.

4. In a large mixing bowl, combine the eggs and heavy cream. Whisk until well blended. Fold in the corn kernels, red onion, and green chili pepper. Season with salt and white pepper to taste and pour the mixture into the prepared ramequins.

5. Place the ramequins in a shallow baking dish and fill the baking dish with water to come halfway up the sides of the ramequins.

6. Set the dish in the center of the preheated oven and bake until the custards are set and the tip of a sharp knife when inserted comes out clean. Remove from the oven and set aside.

7. *To serve:* Toss the salad and place some on each of 4 to 6 individual salad plates. Unmold a warm corn custard in the center of each on top of the greens. Sprinkle the greens with the crumbled bacon and serve at once.

Swiss Cheese Beignets with Chives & Tossed Green Salad

1. Start by making *the beignets:* In a medium saucepan combine the water, butter, and ¼ teaspoon coarse salt. Place over medium heat and bring to a boil. Remove from the heat and immediately add the flour all at once and beat vigorously with a wooden spoon until the flour is thoroughly incorporated.

2. Reduce heat to low, return the saucepan to the heat, and beat the dough for 1–1½ minutes to dry.

3. Transfer the dough to a food processor and with the machine running add the eggs one at a time, processing after each addition until thoroughly combined. Add the cheese and chives and pulse quickly, on and off, to just combine. The dough should be quite sticky.

4. Transfer the dough to a mixing bowl and let cool to room temperature.

5. In a large saucepan heat the oil to 350° on a deep-fry ther-mometer. Drop the dough by heaping teaspoonfuls into the hot oil, 4 to 6 at a time. Cook for 6 minutes or until the beignets have stopped expanding and are nicely browned on all sides. Turn the beignets from time to time in the oil to brown evenly. Remove with a slotted spoon to a double layer of paper towels. Continue to deep-fry in batches of 6 until all the dough is used. Sprinkle with coarse salt.

6. Toss the salad greens with the vinaigrette and divide among 8 individual salad plates. Top each with about 3–4 beignets and serve at once.

THE BEIGNETS

½ cup water

3 tablespoons unsalted butter, softened

Coarse salt

½ cup all-purpose flour

2 large eggs

1 cup grated Swiss cheese, preferably imported

2 tablespoons finely minced fresh chives

4 cups corn oil for deep-frying

THE SALAD

8 cups loosely packed mixed salad greens, including dandelions, young spinach leaves, and arugula

1 recipe Provençale Vinaigrette (page 79)

SERVES 8

Linguine with Mustard Greens & Clams

10 tablespoons olive oil, preferably
    extra-virgin

4 large cloves garlic, peeled and
    sliced

1 pound mustard greens, stemmed,
    washed, and dried on paper
    towels

Salt and freshly ground black
    pepper

1 small fresh hot pepper, sliced, or
    dried, crumbled

½ cup parsley leaves

¼ cup dry white wine

20 littleneck clams, scrubbed clean

¾ pound linguine

SERVES 4

*You may also serve the clams without
their shells. Remove the shells and
discard. Dice the clams and keep
warm in their cooking liquid until
ready to toss with the pasta.*

1. In a large skillet, heat 4 tablespoons olive oil over medium heat. Add 2 of the garlic cloves and cook for 1 minute without browning.

2. Add the mustard greens to the skillet and cook, tossing constantly in the oil, until the leaves begin to wilt. Season with salt and pepper and keep warm.

3. In a large casserole, heat 3 tablespoons olive oil over medium heat. Add the cayenne pepper, remaining garlic, parsley, white wine, and clams. Cover and cook until all the clams have opened; discard those that do not. Keep clams warm in their cooking liquid.

4. In another large casserole, bring plenty of salted water to a boil, add the linguine and cook until just tender, al dente. Immediately add 2 cups cold water to stop further cooking and drain.

5. Transfer the pasta to a serving bowl and toss with the remaining olive oil, clams, clam cooking liquid and warm greens. Taste and correct the seasoning. Serve at once.

Spaghettini with Mustard Greens & Spicy Sausage

P·R·E·P·A·R·A·T·I·O·N

1. In a large heavy skillet heat 1 tablespoon olive oil over medium-high heat. Add the sausages and cook partially covered until nicely browned on all sides. Transfer to a cutting surface and cut crosswise into ¼-inch slices. Reserve.

2. Discard all the fat from the skillet and add 4 tablespoons olive oil. Add the garlic and ⅓ of the mustard greens. Cook, stirring constantly, until the leaves begin to wilt. Add another ⅓ of the greens to the skillet, without removing the previous batch, and cook until the leaves begin to wilt. Add the remaining greens and cook until all the leaves have wilted.

3. Return the sausage to the skillet, together with the black olives, and just heat through. Keep warm.

4. Bring plenty of lightly salted water to a boil in a large casserole. Add the pasta and cook until just tender, al dente. Immediately add 2 cups cold water to the pot to stop further cooking. Drain thoroughly and add to the skillet together with the remaining olive oil. Toss well with the sausage and greens.

5. Taste and correct the seasoning and serve at once directly from the skillet with a bowl of freshly grated Parmesan cheese and a crusty loaf of French bread.

7 tablespoons olive oil, preferably extra-virgin

4 hot Italian sausage links

2 large cloves garlic, peeled and thinly sliced

2 pounds mustard greens, stemmed, washed, and dried on paper towels

16 small black oil-cured olives

Salt

½ pound spaghettini

Freshly ground black pepper

ACCOMPANIMENT

Bowl of freshly grated Parmesan cheese

SERVES 4

PROVENÇALE VINAIGRETTE

In a small jar combine 1 tablespoon olive oil, 2–3 tablespoons red wine vinegar, 2 teaspoons Dijon mustard and 1 clove garlic, crushed. Season with salt and pepper. Cover and shake until smooth.

Variations:
Basic: Omit garlic
Herb: Add 2 tablespoons minced chives, parsley or dill

Warm Mustard Green Salad
with Tomato Salsa

1½ pounds mustard greens, stemmed, washed, and dried on paper towels

3 tablespoons red wine vinegar

4 tablespoons olive oil

¼ cup pine nuts

½ cup finely diced slab bacon, blanched

2 large cloves garlic, peeled and thinly sliced

Salt and freshly ground black pepper

1 recipe tomato salsa (see Corn Crepes with Steamed Asparagus & Spicy Salsa, page 18)

SERVES 4

1. Toss the mustard greens with the red wine vinegar in a large bowl. Set aside.

2. In a large heavy skillet, heat 2 tablespoons olive oil over medium heat. Add the pine nuts and cook, stirring constantly, until lightly browned. Transfer to a side dish and reserve.

3. Add the bacon to the skillet and cook until lightly browned. Remove with a slotted spoon to a side dish.

4. Discard all but 2 tablespoons of fat from the skillet. Add the remaining oil and, when hot, add the sliced garlic and mustard greens. Toss until barely wilted and just warm. Return the bacon and pine nuts to the skillet and season with salt and pepper.

5. Divide the greens mixture among 4 individual salad plates. Top each with a dollop of tomato salsa and serve at once.

Cream of Mustard Greens, Boston Lettuce & Blue Cheese Soup

1. In a heavy 4-quart casserole, melt 3 tablespoons butter over medium heat. Add the leeks and ¼ cup stock. Reduce heat, cover, and braise until tender, about 14 minutes.

2. Add the mustard greens and toss with the leeks until just wilted. Season with salt and pepper. Add the remaining stock and bring to a boil. Reduce heat and simmer, partially covered, for 15 minutes.

3. Strain the soup into a large bowl. Transfer the vegetables to a food processor or blender and puree until smooth. Whisk the pureed vegetables into the strained broth and reserve.

4. Combine the heavy cream and Roquefort in a food processor or blender and puree until smooth. Set aside.

5. Add the remaining butter to the casserole and place over medium heat until melted. Whisk in the flour and cook for 2 minutes without browning. Add the reserved vegetable broth and whisk until well blended.

6. Bring to a boil, add the cream/Roquefort mixture, reduce heat to low, and simmer uncovered for 10 minutes longer. Do not let come to a boil.

7. Add the shredded Boston lettuce and stir until just wilted but still a bit crisp. Taste and correct the seasoning and serve hot.

7 tablespoons unsalted butter

2 large leeks, trimmed of all but 2 inches of greens, finely sliced and rinsed of all sand

6 cups Chicken Stock (page 41) or bouillon

1 pound mustard greens, stemmed, well rinsed, and cut into 1-inch pieces

Salt and freshly ground white pepper

¾–1 cup heavy cream

6 tablespoons Roquefort or other mild blue cheese, crumbled

2 tablespoons all-purpose flour

1 small head Boston lettuce, leaves separated, washed, and shredded

SERVES 6

Gratin of Collard Greens with Garlic & Cheese

Butter

¼ cup homemade bread crumbs

1½ pounds collard greens, stemmed
  and washed thoroughly

Salt

3 tablespoons olive oil

2 large shallots, peeled and finely
  minced

2 large cloves garlic, peeled and
  finely minced

Freshly ground white pepper

6 large cloves garlic, peeled

1½ cups light cream or a mixture
  of heavy cream and milk

4 whole large eggs

½ cup coarsely grated Gruyère or
  Swiss cheese

Large grinding of nutmeg

2 tablespoons freshly grated
  Parmesan cheese

SERVES 6

P·R·E·P·A·R·A·T·I·O·N

1. Preheat oven to 350°.

2. Generously butter a 3-quart oval gratin dish or rectangular baking dish. Sprinkle with the bread crumbs, shaking out the excess, and set aside.

3. Bring plenty of lightly salted water to a boil in a large saucepan. Add the collard greens, cook for 2 minutes, drain, and when cool enough to handle, gently squeeze to remove excess liquid. Finely chop and set aside.

4. In a large skillet, heat the olive oil over medium heat. Add the shallots and minced garlic and cook until soft but not brown. Add the chopped collard greens and cook for 2 minutes. Season with salt and pepper and reserve.

5. Place the whole garlic cloves in a small saucepan with water to cover. Bring to a boil, cook for 1 minute, and drain.

6. Add more water to the saucepan, bring to a boil, add the blanched garlic cloves, and cook for 15 minutes or until tender. Drain and transfer to a food processor or blender together with ¼ cup of the light cream and process until smooth.

7. In a large bowl, combine the eggs, garlic cream, and remaining light cream. Whisk until well blended. Add the collard mixture and Gruyère cheese. Season with salt, pepper, and a large grinding of nutmeg.

8. Pour the mixture into the prepared gratin dish and sprinkle with the Parmesan cheese.

9. Place the gratin dish in a large shallow baking pan. Fill the baking pan with boiling water to come halfway up the sides of the gratin dish. Place in the center of the preheated oven and bake for about 25 minutes or until the custard is set and top is lightly browned. A knife when inserted should come out clean.

10. Remove from the oven and let cool 10 minutes before serving. Serve hot or at room temperature as an accompaniment to grilled meats.

Collard Greens with Anchovy & Garlic Butter

P·R·E·P·A·R·A·T·I·O·N

1. With a sharp knife cut out the entire stem from each collard green leaf and discard. Tear the leaves into 1½-inch pieces and rinse 2 to 3 times in cold water to remove all sand.

2. Bring plenty of lightly salted water to a boil in a large casserole. Add the greens and cook for 2–3 minutes or until just tender. Drain thoroughly in a colander and when cool enough to handle, squeeze gently to remove excess moisture.

3. In a large skillet melt the butter over medium to low heat. Add the garlic, anchovies, and capers and cook for 1 minute or until the anchovies have "melted." Add the collard greens and toss in the butter until just heated through. Taste and correct the seasoning, adding a large grinding of black pepper. Serve at once.

4 pounds collard greens
Salt
6–8 tablespoons unsalted butter
3 large cloves garlic, peeled and
    finely minced
6 anchovy fillets
2 tablespoons tiny capers, drained
Freshly ground black pepper

SERVES 4–6

Baked Salmon Fillets in Sorrel Mayonnaise

SORREL MAYONNAISE

2 cups tightly packed sorrel leaves, stemmed

2 large eggs

2 teaspoons wine vinegar

¾ cup corn or peanut oil

2 tablespoons finely minced scallions

2 tablespoons finely minced fresh parsley

Salt and freshly ground black pepper

Lemon juice to taste

THE SALMON

3 tablespoons unsalted butter, melted

1½ pounds of salmon fillet

Salt and freshly ground white pepper

GARNISH

Sprigs of flat-leaf parsley

SERVES 4

1. *The sorrel mayonnaise:* Wash the sorrel leaves thoroughly under cold water. Place in a medium saucepan with just the water that clings to the leaves and cook over low heat until the sorrel "melts" and is reduced to a soft puree. Place sorrel in a strainer and let cool.

2. In the container of a blender combine the eggs and vinegar. Blend the mixture at high speed for 30 seconds. Reduce speed to low and add the oil by droplets until the sauce is thick and smooth and all the oil has been added. Add the sorrel and blend for 30 seconds.

3. Pour the sauce into a bowl. Add the scallions, parsley, salt, pepper, and lemon juice to taste. Set aside.

4. Preheat oven to 350°.

5. *The salmon:* Place melted butter in a large baking dish and set aside.

6. Cut the salmon crosswise into 4 pieces. Place each salmon piece between 2 sheets of plastic wrap and pound lightly with a cleaver.

7. Place the salmon fillets in the buttered baking dish in a single layer; do not overlap. Sprinkle with salt and white pepper and turn to coat evenly with the melted butter.

8. Set the baking dish in the center of the preheated oven and bake the fillets for 3–4 minutes on each side or until just opaque. Do not overcook.

9. Remove from the oven and gently pull on the skin to remove. Place each salmon fillet on an individual serving plate and spoon the sorrel sauce over them. Garnish each with a sprig of fresh parsley and serve at once.

Country Sorrel Soup

P·R·E·P·A·R·A·T·I·O·N

1. In a heavy 3½-quart casserole, melt the butter over medium heat. Add the onion and cook until soft but not brown.

2. Add the potatoes, sorrel, and 6 cups of chicken stock. Bring to a boil, reduce heat, cover, and simmer 10–15 minutes or until vegetables are very soft.

3. Cool the soup and puree until smooth in a food processor or blender. Return the soup to the casserole. If the soup is too thick, add the remaining chicken stock.

4. Whisk in the optional sour cream and just heat through. Do not let the soup come to a boil. Taste and correct the seasoning, adding lemon juice to taste and a large grinding of pepper.

R·E·M·A·R·K·S

The soup can also be served chilled with a dollop of sour cream, sprinkled with a little zest of either lemon or lime on each portion.

3 tablespoons unsalted butter
1 large onion, peeled and finely minced
3 medium all-purpose potatoes, peeled and cubed
3 cups tightly packed sorrel leaves, stemmed
6–8 cups Chicken Stock (page 41)
½ cup sour cream (optional)
Salt and freshly ground white pepper
Lemon juice to taste

SERVES 6

BURPEE'S

PEAS

The very first crop that goes into my garden in spring is a row of peas.

When I was a child, shelling peas was one of my almost daily chores—one that I did not mind too much since I would munch on almost as many as I would shell. Possibly because of the work involved, I loved peas more than any other vegetable. A plateful of freshly cooked sweet peas, sometimes sautéed with bits of smoked ham or air-cured prosciutto, was a favorite first course at our house. Indeed, when in season, cooked peas found their way into many preparations where their bright green color, unique texture, and delicate sweet taste would mark each dish with a sign of spring. My mother's recipe of the Viennese *risi bisi,* in which a simple but flavorful pilaf of rice is laced with peas and parsley, is still one of my favorite accompaniments to meats and poultry, as is the classic *salade Russe,* in which fresh-cooked peas, carrots, beans, and potatoes are bound together in a flavorful mayonnaise. In fact, I find that peas are good in just about everything. They are delicious in pasta dishes, in a sauté of veal with mushrooms (see page 92), in cold dishes such as the chicken salad on page 96, and braised with small white onions or hearts of Boston lettuce.

The reason peas available from a greengrocer are so seldom truly fresh is that the sugar they contain turns to starch within hours of picking. In order to enjoy this vegetable at its best, you are almost forced to grow your own. Since peas demand little care in the garden, they are well worth the effort. And there is no shortage of varieties to choose from. Among the best is Maestro; early and highly productive, it is resistant to powdery mildew and other diseases that affect peas. The true soup pea is Alaska, which lends itself to drying and winter use.

Another lovely garden pea is the snow pea, which has a crunchy and delicious flat pod and is harvested before the little peas develop. Although primarily used in Chinese and other Oriental stir-fries, snow peas are now used creatively in many Western dishes and salads. Simply steamed, they are a wonderful

HOMEMADE MAYONNAISE

In a blender combine 1 whole egg, 1 egg yolk, 2–3 teaspoons lemon juice or vinegar, and salt and white pepper to taste. With blender at top speed, add ¾ cup vegetable oil by droplets until mixture begins to thicken. Add remaining oil in a steady stream until incorporated. Keep in refrigerator in tightly covered jar. Makes 1¼ cups.

accompaniment to a variety of meats, poultry, and fish. They can be combined with other spring vegetables in a colorful stir-fry, or served by themselves, either sautéed or blanched and buttered. Oregon Sugar Pod II is a delicious and particularly disease-resistant variety. Although snow peas are available in many markets throughout the year, they are quite expensive and often lack that crunchy freshness that makes the garden vegetable so unique.

In recent years the new snap peas have become increasingly popular, and it is easy to see why. They can be eaten pod and all, or the pods can be shelled for the full-size peas within. Unlike snow peas, the pods are thick and fleshy, excellent raw along with a dip, on a relish tray, or eaten alone as a snack. The first variety to be introduced was Sugar Snap, which produces juicy three-inch-long pods, but several varieties have recently become available, including Burpee's Snappy, which has longer, shapelier pods.

S·T·O·R·A·G·E

Fresh peas, snow peas, and snap peas can be stored successfully for three to four days in the refrigerator in a plastic bag. Shell the peas just before cooking. Shelled garden peas can be frozen, although they do not retain their crisp texture.

G·A·R·D·E·N·I·N·G

I usually make a few separate plantings at two- to three-week intervals starting in very early spring. Peas cannot tolerate heat, so plan for the last spring sowing to mature before daytime temperatures average above 75°. Additional plantings can be made in midsummer for harvest during fall, even after light frosts. Friends in southern California tell me that their pea crops do best in winter.

Before sowing, fertilize soil with Burpee fertilizer and add a granular inoculant of nitrogen-fixing bacteria, which enables

roots of peas and other legumes to convert nitrogen from the air into a useful plant nutrient. Chicken-wire cages or garden netting provide excellent support for tall-growing varieties.

H · A · R · V · E · S · T · I · N · G

For the sweetest peas, pick pods just before time for cooking. The safest way to harvest is to hold the pod stem in one hand and the pod itself in the other. Then break. Merely yanking or twisting with one hand may uproot the plant.

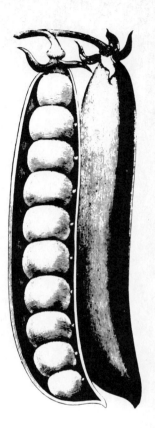

Sauté of Calf's Liver with Peas, Onions & Shiitake Mushrooms

P·R·E·P·A·R·A·T·I·O·N

1 pound calf's liver, thinly sliced

6–8 dry shiitake mushrooms, stems removed

8 tablespoons unsalted butter

2 teaspoons olive oil

2 large Bermuda onions, peeled, quartered, and thinly sliced

2 teaspoons granulated sugar

Salt and freshly ground white pepper

1 pound fresh peas (about 1 cup shelled)

Flour for dredging

SERVES 4

1. Cut the liver crosswise into ¼-inch strips and reserve.

2. Soak the shiitake mushrooms in warm water to cover for 30 minutes or until soft. Drain and cut crosswise into ¼-inch slices. Set aside.

3. In a large heavy skillet heat 3 tablespoons butter and 1 teaspoon oil over medium heat. Add the onions, sprinkle with 1 teaspoon sugar, season with salt and pepper, and cook for 30 minutes, stirring often, until the onions are soft and nicely browned. Remove from the skillet to a side dish and reserve.

4. Add another tablespoon of butter to the skillet. Add the sliced mushrooms, quickly sauté for 1 minute, and add to the reserved onions.

5. In a small saucepan combine the peas with water to cover, 2 tablespoons butter, the remaining sugar, and salt and pepper to taste. Cook the peas for 3 minutes or until just tender. Do not overcook. Drain and reserve.

6. Sprinkle the liver slices lightly with flour and season with pepper. Do not salt.

7. Heat the remaining butter and oil in a large heavy skillet over high heat. Add the calf's liver and cook quickly until it just loses its pink color, about 1 minute. Do not overcook.

8. Immediately remove the pan from the heat, season lightly with salt, and add the onion/mushroom mixture together with the peas. Return to low heat and toss the liver gently to just heat through. Correct the seasoning and serve at once.

Pea, Carrot, Potato & Scallop Salad in Green Mayonnaise

1. Place peas in a saucepan with water to cover. Add the sugar and a pinch of salt. Bring to a boil, reduce heat, and cook 3–4 minutes or until just tender. Drain and transfer to a large mixing bowl.

2. Bring lightly salted water to a boil in a vegetable steamer. Add the carrots, cover, and steam until just tender. Remove and set aside. Add the potatoes, cover, and steam until just tender. Add the potatoes and carrots to the bowl containing the peas. Set aside.

3. To the vegetable steamer, add the scallops, cover, and steam 2–3 minutes or until they just turn opaque. Transfer to the mixing bowl and toss with the vegetables.

4. In a food processor or blender, combine the mayonnaise, mustard, parsley, and scallions and puree until smooth. Taste and correct the seasoning.

5. Pour the green mayonnaise over the vegetables and scallops and toss gently. Sprinkle with the chives and chill for 6–12 hours before serving.

6. *To serve:* Toss the arugula leaves in a little olive oil and vinegar. Place some of the arugula on individual salad plates. Top with the vegetable and scallop salad and serve at once.

2 pounds fresh peas (about 2 cups shelled)

1 teaspoon granulated sugar

Salt

2 medium carrots, peeled and cut into ½-inch cubes

3 medium red potatoes, peeled and cut into ½-inch cubes

½ pound small bay scallops

1 cup Homemade Mayonnaise, (page 88)

2 teaspoons Dijon mustard

½ cup fresh parsley leaves

2 tablespoons minced scallions

Freshly ground black pepper

3 tablespoons finely minced fresh chives

THE SALAD GREENS

2 bunches fresh arugula, stemmed, washed, and dried on paper towels

4 tablespoons olive oil, preferably extra-virgin

1 tablespoon red wine vinegar

SERVES 4–6

Spring Veal Ragout à la Française

3 pounds veal shoulder, cut into
   1½-inch cubes
1 tablespoon peanut oil
4 tablespoons unsalted butter
Salt and freshly ground white
   pepper
Sprinkling of all-purpose flour
2 cups Chicken Stock (page 41)
2 small onions, peeled
1 Bouquet Garni (page 92)
½ pound fresh mushrooms, wiped,
   stemmed, and quartered
1 cup Crème Fraîche (page 55) or
   heavy cream
1 recipe Beurre Manié (page 20)
1 cup cooked fresh peas

GARNISH

2–3 tablespoons finely minced fresh
   parsley
¼ cup cooked fresh peas

SERVES 6

BOUQUET GARNI

To compose Bouquet Garni, tie
together 2–3 sprigs Italian parsley, 1
small celery stalk, 1 bay leaf and 1
large sprig thyme.

P·R·E·P·A·R·A·T·I·O·N

1. Preheat oven to 350°. Dry the veal thoroughly on paper towels and set aside.

2. In a large heavy skillet, heat the oil and 2 tablespoons of the butter over medium-high heat. Add the veal cubes a few at a time without crowding the pan and sauté until nicely browned on all sides. Transfer with a slotted spoon to a side dish and continue sautéeing until all the veal is browned. Season with salt and pepper.

3. Discard the fat from the skillet and return all the veal to the pan. Sprinkle lightly with flour and toss the meat until lightly glazed. Remove the veal to a heavy casserole or Dutch oven and reserve.

4. Add the stock to the skillet, bring to a boil, and scrape the bottom of the pan well. Pour over the veal, add the onions and bouquet garni, and cover the casserole tightly. Place in the center of the preheated oven and braise for 1 hour 20 minutes or until tender.

5. While the meat is braising, prepare *the mushrooms:* In a medium skillet heat the remaining butter over medium-high heat. Add the mushrooms and sauté quickly, shaking the pan back and forth until nicely browned. Season with salt and pepper and reserve.

6. When the veal is done, remove the meat with a slotted spoon to a side dish and discard the onions and bouquet garni. Degrease the pan juices carefully and return them to the casserole.

7. Place the casserole with the pan juices over high heat. Add the crème fraîche or heavy cream, bring to a boil, and reduce slightly. Whisk in bits of beurre manié until sauce heavily coats a spoon.

8. Return the veal to the casserole together with the sautéed mushrooms and cooked peas and just heat through. Taste and correct the seasoning.

9. Spoon the ragout into a serving dish, sprinkle with the parsley and some cooked peas, and serve at once with a crusty loaf of French bread.

Sugar Snap Pea & Carrot Salad

P·R·E·P·A·R·A·T·I·O·N

1. Bring lightly salted water to a boil in a vegetable steamer, add the snap peas, cover, and steam for 3–5 minutes or until crisp-tender. Remove and run under cold water to stop further cooking. Drain on paper towels. Place in a salad bowl and set aside.

2. Add the carrots to the steamer, cover, and steam for 2 minutes. Add to the salad bowl with the peas, cover, and chill.

3. Combine the scallions, dill, parsley, vinegar, olive oil, and walnuts in a food processor or blender and puree until smooth. Season with salt and pepper to taste and pour the dressing over the peas and carrots. Cover and chill for at least 2 hours.

4. Just before serving, toss the salad with the radishes and correct the seasoning. Serve slightly chilled.

1½ pounds Sugar Snap peas, strings removed
Salt
4 medium carrots, peeled and cut into matchsticks (¼ by ¼ by 1½ inches)
¾ cup finely minced scallions
4 tablespoons finely minced fresh dill
4 tablespoons finely minced fresh parsley
5 tablespoons white wine vinegar
9 tablespoons olive oil
1½ ounces walnut pieces
Freshly ground black pepper
½ cup thinly sliced radishes

SERVES 6

Sugar Snap Pea Salad with Lemon & Scallion Vinaigrette

1½ pounds Sugar Snap peas,
    strings removed
Salt
Juice of 1 large lemon
6 tablespoons olive oil
1 tablespoon Dijon mustard
2 teaspoons granulated sugar
4 tablespoons finely minced
    scallions
Freshly ground white pepper

SERVES 6

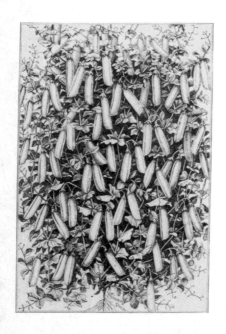

P·R·E·P·A·R·A·T·I·O·N

1. Bring lightly salted water to a boil in a vegetable steamer, add the snap peas, cover, and steam for 3–5 minutes or until crisp-tender. Remove and run under cold water to stop further cooking. Drain on paper towels, place in a salad bowl, and chill.

2. In a small jar combine the lemon juice, olive oil, mustard, and sugar. Cover the jar and shake until the dressing is smooth and well blended. Add the scallions and season with salt and pepper to taste. The dressing should have a definite sweet-sour taste.

3. Pour the dressing over the snap peas, cover, and chill for at least 2 hours. Serve slightly chilled.

V·A·R·I·A·T·I·O·N

You may turn the salad into a luncheon dish simply by adding ¼ cup finely diced Gruyère or Swiss cheese and ¼ cup finely diced smoked ham. Serve chilled on leaves of mixed garden greens accompanied by a crusty loaf of French bread.

Sauté of Chicken in Vinegar Garlic Sauce

P·R·E·P·A·R·A·T·I·O·N

1. In a heavy 12-inch skillet, melt 2 tablespoons butter over medium-high heat. Add the mushrooms and sauté quickly until nicely browned. Season with salt and pepper. Remove to a side dish and reserve.

2. Dry the chicken pieces thoroughly on paper towels.

3. Add 2 more tablespoons of butter and 1 teaspoon of oil to the skillet. When hot, add the chicken pieces without crowding the pan and sauté quickly on all sides until nicely browned. If necessary, partially cover the skillet to prevent splattering. Transfer to a side dish, season with salt and pepper, and reserve.

4. Degrease the pan juices and reserve. Add the remaining butter to the skillet and reduce heat to medium. Add garlic and cook for 30 seconds, stirring constantly and being careful not to burn. Add vinegar and reduce to a glaze.

5. Return the chicken pieces and their juices to the skillet. Reduce heat and add 2 tablespoons chicken stock and the fresh thyme. Cover and simmer for 30–35 minutes or until the chicken is done. If during cooking the pan juices run dry, add the remaining stock.

6. Add the cream, sautéed mushrooms, and peas to the skillet. Continue cooking another 2–3 minutes or until vegetables are heated through and sauce lightly coats a spoon.

7. Taste and correct the seasoning. Transfer the chicken and vegetables to a serving platter. Spoon sauce over and sprinkle with minced chives. Serve hot, accompanied by thin buttered noodles.

6 tablespoons unsalted butter

8 medium fresh mushrooms, wiped, trimmed, and cut into ¼-inch dice

Salt and freshly ground black pepper

6 small whole chicken legs, from 2½- to 3-pound chickens, cut in half at joint separating the thigh and drumstick

1 teaspoon peanut oil

3 medium cloves garlic, peeled and thinly sliced

¼ cup red wine vinegar, preferably sherry

½ cup Chicken Stock (page 41) or bouillon

1 tablespoon fresh thyme

3–4 tablespoons heavy cream

1 cup cooked fresh peas

GARNISH

2–3 tablespoons finely minced fresh chives

SERVES 4–6

Dilled Chicken Salad with Peas & Asparagus

4 cups Chicken Stock (page 41) or
  bouillon

3 whole chicken breasts, boned,
  skinned, and cut in half

1 large carrot, peeled and cut into
  1/2-inch dice

1/2 pound fresh asparagus, peeled
  and cut into 3/4-inch pieces

1 cup cooked fresh peas

2 whole large eggs

1 large egg yolk

1 tablespoon Dijon mustard

Juice of 1/2 lemon

2 tablespoons red wine vinegar

3/4–1 cup peanut oil

Salt and freshly ground black
  pepper

1/3 cup finely diced scallions

3–4 tablespoons finely minced fresh
  dill

GARNISH

Leaves of young Boston lettuce

12 ripe cherry tomatoes, cut in half

12 small black oil-cured olives

SERVES 6–8

1. In a large saucepan heat the chicken broth over medium heat. Add the chicken breasts 2 or 3 pieces at a time, reduce heat to low, and poach for 6–8 minutes. Remove to a side dish and reserve. Continue poaching the remaining chicken breasts and set aside.

2. Set a steamer rack in the saucepan over the broth, add the carrot, cover, and steam until just tender. Transfer to a salad bowl.

3. Remove the steamer rack and add the asparagus to the broth. Cook until just tender, drain, and add to the salad bowl together with the peas.

4. Cut the chicken breasts into 3/4-inch cubes and add to the salad bowl. Set aside.

5. In the container of a blender combine the eggs, yolk, mustard, lemon juice, and vinegar. Blend at high speed for 30 seconds and then with the machine still at top speed start adding the oil by droplets. As the mayonnaise begins to thicken, add the remaining oil in a slow steady stream. Season with salt and pepper and spoon over the chicken mixture.

6. Add the scallions and dill and toss the salad gently until well blended.

7. Chill the salad for at least 24 hours before serving. Bring the salad partially back to room temperature and taste and correct the seasoning, adding a large grinding of pepper and possibly another dash of vinegar. Serve slightly chilled on a bed of young Boston lettuce leaves, garnished with halved cherry tomatoes and black olives.

Pasta with Pink Tomato Sauce & Julienne of Spring Vegetables

If you cannot get a red pepper, use 1 cup of steamed broccoli florets and add to the cooked pasta. The dish will have a lovely color and texture.

P·R·E·P·A·R·A·T·I·O·N

1. In a heavy 10-inch skillet, heat the olive oil over low heat. Add the zucchini and red pepper and cook for 4–5 minutes or until just tender. Reserve.

2. Bring plenty of lightly salted water to a boil in a large casserole. Add the ziti and cook until just tender.

3. While the ziti are cooking, melt the butter in a medium saucepan over low heat. Add the ham and sauté for 1–2 minutes without browning. Add the peas, tomato sauce, and cream and just heat through. Keep warm.

4. When the ziti are done, immediately add 2 cups cold water to the casserole to stop further cooking. Drain and place in a large serving bowl. Add the zucchini/pepper mixture and the pea/tomato sauce mixture and toss gently. Add a large grinding of black pepper and the julienne of basil. Sprinkle with the Parmesan and serve at once.

3 tablespoons olive oil, preferably extra-virgin

2 small zucchini, cut into julienne strips (¼ by 1½ inches), avoiding as much of the seedy center as possible

1 red bell pepper, cored, seeded, quartered, and cut into ¼-inch strips

Salt

½ pound ziti

3 tablespoons unsalted butter

½ cup finely diced smoked ham

1 cup cooked fresh peas

1½ cups Quick Tomato Sauce (page 38)

½ cup heavy cream

Freshly ground black pepper

⅓ cup julienne of fresh basil leaves

4 tablespoons freshly grated Parmesan cheese

SERVES 4

Cream of Fresh Pea Soup
with Mint

5 tablespoons unsalted butter

1 small onion, peeled and finely minced

3 pounds fresh peas (about 3 cups shelled)

6 cups Chicken Stock (page 41) or bouillon

2½ tablespoons all-purpose flour

½ cup Crème Fraîche (page 57) or sour cream

Salt and freshly ground white pepper

1 cup cooked fresh peas

2–3 tablespoons finely minced fresh mint

GARNISH

Tiny leaves of fresh mint

SERVES 6

P·R·E·P·A·R·A·T·I·O·N

1. In a large casserole melt 2 tablespoons butter over medium heat. Add the onion and cook until soft but not browned.

2. Add the peas and toss with the butter and onion. Add the chicken stock, bring to a boil, reduce heat, and simmer, partially covered, for 25 minutes or until peas are quite tender.

3. Strain the soup, setting aside the broth.

4. Transfer the cooked peas to the work bowl of a food processor and puree until smooth. Pass the pureed peas through a fine sieve, add to the reserved broth, and whisk until well blended. Set aside.

5. In the same casserole, melt the remaining butter over medium heat. Add the flour and whisk constantly for 2–3 minutes until the mixture turns a light hazelnut brown. Be careful not to burn. Add the broth-pea puree mixture all at once and whisk until the mixture begins to thicken. Reduce heat and simmer for 10 minutes.

6. Whisk in the crème fraîche or sour cream, taste and correct the seasoning, and just heat through. Do not let come to a boil. Just before serving add the cooked peas and minced fresh mint. Serve at once, garnished with tiny leaves of fresh mint.

Sauté of Snow Peas with Scallops & Fresh Coriander

P·R·E·P·A·R·A·T·I·O·N

1. Dry the scallops thoroughly on paper towels. Season with salt and pepper. Dredge lightly with flour, shaking off the excess.

2. In a large heavy skillet, heat the butter with 1 tablespoon of the oil over medium heat. Add the garlic and when nicely browned remove and discard. Raise heat to high, add the scallops without crowding the pan, and sauté until nicely browned on both sides. Remove from the skillet to a side dish and reserve.

3. In another large skillet, heat the remaining peanut oil over medium-high heat. Add the snow peas and sprinkle with the sugar. Toss in the hot oil until glazed. Add the sherry and water and cook until snow peas are just tender and liquid is reduced and syrupy.

4. Add the sautéed scallops to the skillet and toss gently to just heat through. Taste and correct the seasoning, sprinkle with the fresh coriander, and serve as an appetizer or as a simple main course accompanied by buttered fettuccine.

1½ pounds fresh small sea scallops
Salt and freshly ground black pepper
All-purpose flour for dredging
2 tablespoons unsalted butter
2 tablespoons peanut oil
2 large cloves garlic, peeled and crushed
40 snow peas, strings removed
1 teaspoon granulated sugar
2 tablespoons dry sherry
2 tablespoons water
2 tablespoons finely minced fresh coriander (cilantro)

SERVES 4–5

BURPEE'S

SPINACH

Spinach is possibly the most versatile of all greens. Its wonderful bright green color, subtle but assertive taste, and interesting texture have inspired many classic preparations. Dishes called *alla Fiorentina* always include spinach, either as a bed for sautéed meats or in stuffings. The all-American spinach and bacon salad makes a most enjoyable year-round starter, as does a well-flavored spinach soup. Spinach pasta and crepes owe their attractive color to spinach's verdant leaves; a Provençale Mayonnaise (see page 16) would be incomplete without them. And there is no other green that blends as well into stuffings, or is so compatible in custards and many other egg dishes.

When I was growing up, spinach was braised and served *alla Catalane* with diced sautéed bacon, sautéed pine nuts, and sultana raisins. It was always, and still is, one of my favorite ways to prepare this vegetable. The claim that children do not like spinach surprises me since there are few greens that taste as delicious when simply prepared, either buttered or pureed and then enriched with fresh butter and a touch of cream.

While fresh spinach is available practically the entire year in supermarkets and greengrocers, it is a far cry from the tender leafy green of the kitchen garden. In supermarkets spinach is often sold in cellophane bags. Here you find mostly stems and broken leaves that lend themselves only to cooked preparations. In recent years, more and more truly fresh spinach has become available at good greengrocers, allowing cooks to use it raw in a variety of interesting salads as well as in cooking.

Much of the summer spinach found in West Coast supermarkets is New Zealand spinach, which has elongated thin leaves and is not related to true spinach. Friends of mine in southern California, where temperatures are too warm for standard spinach, have excellent luck with the New Zealand because it is heat-resistant. I like it raw in salads (young leaves are best) and find it useful in preparations such as spinach pasta or crepes.

For many gardeners the excitement that marks the beginning of a new growing season starts with the planting of spinach.

Young leaves become part of the late-spring salad bowl within six to seven weeks of my first sowing.

Spinach is extremely gritty and takes several soakings in lukewarm water before it is ready to be cooked. Once thoroughly washed the spinach should be stemmed unless it is very young, in which case the tiny stems add a nice texture to the cooked greens. I like to cook spinach either in a saucepan or a skillet with a very small amount of water, preferably only the water that clings to the leaves after washing. I steam spinach only when it is to be used for a stuffing or as a coloring agent for a mayonnaise or pasta. Spinach can absorb an extraordinary amount of butter, which is the reason why simply buttered spinach is so sinfully delicious.

S·T·O·R·A·G·E

Spinach will keep for two to three days refrigerated in a plastic bag. If it is to be used in a salad it should be spun dry in a salad spinner and served as soon as possible.

G·A·R·D·E·N·I·N·G

Timing is of the essence with this otherwise undemanding green. When daytime temperatures rise much above 75°, spinach plants bolt—that is, they rush into flower and then quickly go to seed, ending their production of harvestable leaves.

I find that the key to success is to start sowing seeds directly in the garden as soon as the soil is workable in early spring. Even if plants are struck by late frost, the hardy foliage will not be damaged significantly. Sow successive crops every couple of weeks, stopping five or six weeks before the first hot weather is expected to arrive. Resume sowing in late summer for additional picking in fall. In regions where winters are warm, it is best to begin sowing in autumn for productive crops in winter and spring. Be sure to use fresh spinach seeds each year.

Water frequently enough to keep soil evenly moist at all

times, and fertilize when young plants become about three inches tall. Spinach is ready for harvest when the largest leaves reach six to eight inches in length. Use a sharp knife to cut away the entire plant near ground level or just pick leaves from several plants and let the others continue to grow.

Spinach with crinkled leaves, known as savoy spinach, has a thicker, more appealing texture and also richer green color than smooth-leaved types. One of my favorite varieties is Bloomsdale Longstanding, which is slow to bolt and sports beautifully savoyed leaves. Also excellent is Avon Hybrid, a fast-growing spinach with semi-crinkled foliage that is large and succulent.

New Zealand spinach is sensitive to cold, so wait until all danger of frost has passed before sowing seeds in the garden. Germination will be hastened if seeds are soaked in water overnight just prior to planting. To encourage thick growth, pinch back the main runners as soon as they begin to spread. Water whenever the top inch of soil becomes dry, and fertilize periodically throughout the season. Picking can begin about two months after sowing. For continuous harvests during summer, snip leaves as needed (but at least once a week), allowing new growth to replace whatever is cut.

Spinach & Spring Vegetable Soup

P·R·E·P·A·R·A·T·I·O·N

1 pound fresh asparagus, trimmed

5 tablespoons unsalted butter

2 small leeks, trimmed of all but 2 inches of greens, thinly sliced and well washed

6 cups Chicken Stock (page 41) or bouillon

1 pound fresh spinach, stemmed, washed, and dried

2½ tablespoons all-purpose flour

Salt and freshly ground white pepper

1 pound fresh peas (about 1 cup shelled)

½–¾ cup heavy cream

Heart of a Boston or Bibb lettuce, leaves separated, washed, and dried

GARNISH

Sprinkling of chives or watercress leaves

SERVES 6

1. Peel the asparagus stalks and cut into 1-inch pieces, reserving the tips.

2. In a heavy 3-quart saucepan heat 2 tablespoons butter. Add the leeks and a little stock. Cover and simmer until tender. Add the remaining stock, the diced asparagus stalks, and bring to a boil. Cook until the asparagus is very tender. Add 2 cups of spinach leaves and cook until tender or for about another 5 minutes. Cool the soup and puree in the food processor or blender until very smooth. Set aside.

3. In a 3½-quart casserole heat the remaining butter. Add the flour and whisk until well blended. Do not brown. Whisk in the pureed soup and bring to a boil. Season carefully with salt and pepper.

4. Add the peas and cook for 4–5 minutes or until barely tender. Add the asparagus tips and cook until tender.

5. Add the heavy cream. Just before serving add the remaining spinach and the lettuce leaves and heat the soup without letting it come to a boil. The lettuce should remain somewhat crisp. Taste and correct the seasoning and serve the soup garnished with a sprinkling of chives and/or a few watercress leaves.

R·E·M·A·R·K·S

This soup is best when prepared a day in advance and reheated.

Spinach & Mushroom Salad with Creamy Sesame Dressing

1. Combine the spinach, onion, and mushrooms in a large serving bowl. Cover and chill.

2. In a medium mixing bowl, combine the egg yolk, vinegar, sugar, and garlic. Whisk until well blended.

3. Start adding the oil by droplets to the egg yolk mixture, whisking constantly until the mixture becomes creamy. Continue to add the oil in a slow steady stream, still whisking constantly, until the mixture thickens. Season with salt and pepper.

4. Pour about 10–12 tablespoons of the dressing over the spinach salad. Toss gently, correct the seasoning, and serve at once.

R·E·M·A·R·K·S

The dressing can be made well ahead of time and kept refrigerated. Whisk the dressing often and again just before serving.

6 ounces fresh young spinach leaves (about 6 cups), stemmed, washed, and dried on paper towels

3 tablespoons thinly sliced red onion

6 medium fresh mushrooms, trimmed and thinly sliced

1 teaspoon egg yolk

2 tablespoons red wine vinegar

1 teaspoon granulated sugar

1 medium clove garlic, peeled and mashed

½ cup peanut oil, mixed with 2 tablespoons sesame oil

Salt and freshly ground black pepper

SERVES 4–5

Savory Spinach Pancakes

2 cups fresh spinach leaves,
  stemmed, washed, and steamed

1 cup buttermilk

1 teaspoon grated raw onion

2 large eggs, lightly beaten

1 cup all-purpose flour

1 teaspoon baking powder

10–12 tablespoons unsalted butter,
  melted

Salt and freshly ground black
  pepper

GARNISH

Smoked fish

Melted unsalted butter

MAKES 20–24 PANCAKES

P·R·E·P·A·R·A·T·I·O·N

1. Preheat oven to 200°.

2. Squeeze out excess liquid from the spinach. Transfer the cooked spinach to a food processor or blender together with the buttermilk and process until spinach is finely chopped. Add the onion and eggs and pulse on and off to combine. Set aside.

3. Sift together the flour and baking powder into a medium mixing bowl. Add the spinach mixture and 4 tablespoons melted butter and whisk until well blended. Season with salt and pepper and let the batter rest for 1 hour.

4. In a medium skillet heat 2 tablespoons of the butter over medium heat. Add the batter to the skillet by the tablespoonful without crowding the pan. You will have to cook the pancakes in batches, about 6 per batch. Cook until the bottom is lightly browned, turn over carefully with a spatula, and cook until the other side is lightly browned.

5. Remove from the skillet and transfer to a baking sheet. Place in the preheated oven and keep warm while cooking the remaining pancakes.

6. Continue to cook more pancakes, adding 2 tablespoons of butter to the skillet for each batch. After a couple of batches, wipe skillet clean with paper towels and begin again.

7. To serve, sprinkle the warm pancakes with freshly ground black pepper, top with smoked fish, and drizzle with a little melted butter. Serve at once.

R·E·M·A·R·K·S

The warm pancakes are equally delicious topped with a dollop of sour cream and a few grains of salmon caviar.

Spinach alla Catalane

Here is a quick and delicious stir-fry of spinach. It is a typical recipe of the Catalan region of Spain. The pine nuts are a traditional garnish and give the dish its particular flavor and texture, but the recipe can be made successfully without them.

P·R·E·P·A·R·A·T·I·O·N

1. Bring plenty of lightly salted water to a boil in a large casserole. Add the spinach and cook for 3–5 minutes or until just wilted. Drain and when cool enough to handle, squeeze a little at a time to remove all excess liquid.

2. In a small saucepan, combine the raisins and water to cover. Bring to a boil, drain, and set aside.

3. Heat the oil in a large heavy skillet. Add the pine nuts and cook over low heat until lightly browned. Transfer to a side dish with a slotted spoon.

4. Add the butter to the skillet together with the sliced garlic. Cook for 1 minute without browning. Stir in the ham, spinach, and raisins and cook until all the moisture has evaporated.

5. Add the pine nuts, correct the seasoning, adding a large grinding of pepper, and serve immediately, accompanied by a side dish of fried French bread slices.

3 pounds fresh spinach, stemmed and washed thoroughly
Salt
2–3 tablespoons dark raisins
1 tablespoon olive oil, preferably extra-virgin
2 tablespoons pine nuts
4 tablespoons unsalted butter
2 medium cloves garlic, peeled and thinly sliced
½ cup finely diced smoked ham
Freshly ground black pepper

ACCOMPANIMENT

Slices of French bread fried in olive oil

SERVES 6

Spinach, Scallion & Cheese Omelette

The following recipe is for 2 individual omelettes.

---

4 tablespoons unsalted butter

1 cup tightly packed fresh spinach leaves, stemmed, washed, and dried on paper towels

2 to 3 tablespoons finely minced fresh scallions

Salt and freshly ground white pepper

5–6 large eggs

1 teaspoon fresh thyme leaves

Drops of Tabasco sauce

3 tablespoons feta cheese, crumbled

ACCOMPANIMENT

Rashers of crisp bacon

SERVES 2

1. In a medium skillet, melt 2 tablespoons butter over medium heat. Add the spinach and scallions and toss gently in the butter until the spinach has just wilted. Do not overcook. Season with salt and pepper and set aside.

2. Combine the eggs and thyme in a large bowl. Whisk until well blended and season with salt, pepper, and a dash of Tabasco.

3. In a heavy 8-inch omelette pan, preferably nonstick, heat 1 tablespoon butter over medium-high heat. When butter is hot and the foam begins to subside, add half the egg mixture. Stir the eggs with the back of a fork until the eggs form a thick mass to cover the bottom of the skillet. Cook 1–2 minutes to let settle. Sprinkle with half of the spinach mixture and half the feta cheese.

4. Tilt the pan away from you and with the aid of a spatula fold ⅓ of the omelette—the part farthest away from you—onto itself and toward the center of the pan. Prod the part closest to you, pushing the omelette toward the far end of the skillet. Jerk the pan roughly so that the omelette completely rolls onto itself to form an oval.

5. Turn the omelette onto a plate and keep warm while making the second omelette, again buttering the skillet, etc.

6. Serve at once with a crisp rasher of bacon.

Braised Spinach in Yogurt Sauce

P·R·E·P·A·R·A·T·I·O·N

1. Place the cumin and coriander seeds in a dry heavy skillet over medium heat. Shake pan back and forth until seeds have lightly browned and become fragrant. Set aside.

2. Bring water to a boil in a small saucepan. Add the potatoes, reduce heat, and simmer until tender, about 20–25 minutes. Remove from the heat and let cool completely in the cooking liquid. Peel and cut into ¾-inch cubes. Reserve.

3. In a heavy 10-inch skillet, heat the butter and 2 teaspoons olive oil over medium-high heat. Add the potatoes and cook 2–3 minutes, until the potatoes start to brown, stirring often. Season with salt and pepper. Reduce heat to medium and cook 5 minutes more until nicely browned on all sides. Set aside.

4. *Braise the spinach in 3 batches:* In a heavy 12-inch skillet heat 2 tablespoons olive oil over medium heat. Add 1 sliced garlic clove and when lightly browned add ⅓ of the spinach leaves. Toss them in the oil until just wilted. Transfer the spinach to a colander, pressing lightly to remove most of the excess liquid. Continue cooking the remaining spinach, adding 2 tablespoons oil and 1 sliced garlic clove to the skillet for each batch. Return all the spinach to the skillet. Season with salt, pepper, cumin, and coriander. Cook for 2 minutes, removing any excess water with a large spoon.

5. Add the sautéed potatoes and yogurt and cook for 2 minutes, or until the yogurt is reduced and absorbed by the spinach. Add the mint or dill. Taste and correct the seasoning and serve hot.

1 teaspoon cumin seeds
½ teaspoon coriander seeds
2 medium red potatoes (about 12 ounces), unpeeled
2 tablespoons unsalted butter
6 tablespoons plus 2 teaspoons olive oil
Salt and freshly ground black pepper
3 large cloves garlic, peeled and finely sliced
2 pounds fresh spinach, stemmed, washed, and dried
1 cup yogurt
2 tablespoons finely minced fresh mint or dill

SERVES 4–6

Spinach & Goat Cheese Tart

P·R·E·P·A·R·A·T·I·O·N

1 10-inch prebaked Basic Tart
  Shell (page 111) in a porcelain
  quiche dish

5 tablespoons olive oil, preferably
  extra-virgin

2 medium cloves garlic, peeled and
  thinly sliced

8 ounces fresh spinach, stemmed,
  washed, and dried

Salt and freshly ground black
  pepper

6 ounces mild goat cheese, domestic
  or imported

1¼ cups Crème Fraîche (page 55)
  or heavy cream

4 large eggs

3–4 tablespoons freshly grated
  Parmesan cheese

1 tablespoon finely minced fresh
  thyme leaves

1 teaspoon finely minced fresh
  rosemary leaves

GARNISH (OPTIONAL)

4–6 ripe Italian plum tomatoes, cut
  crosswise into ¼-inch slices

Freshly ground black pepper

1 teaspoon fresh thyme leaves

12–16 fresh rosemary leaves

12–16 small black oil-cured olives

ACCOMPANIMENT

Thin slices of a hard, nicely spiced
  salami

SERVES 6–8

1. Preheat oven to 375°.

2. In a heavy 10-inch skillet heat 3 tablespoons olive oil over medium heat. Add the sliced garlic and stir constantly until golden. Remove the garlic with a slotted spoon and discard.

3. Reduce the heat to low. Add the spinach to the skillet, tossing it in the olive oil to coat the leaves. Season with salt and pepper, cover, and cook until the spinach just wilts, stirring often. Transfer the spinach to a colander, pressing lightly to remove most of the excess liquid. Set aside.

4. In a food processor or blender, combine the goat cheese, crème fraîche, eggs, Parmesan, thyme, and rosemary. Season lightly with salt and pepper. Process until very smooth. Set aside.

5. Distribute the drained spinach evenly over the bottom of the prebaked tart shell. Pour the goat cheese mixture over the spinach. Bake in the center of the preheated oven for 30–35 minutes or until set and golden brown. A toothpick when inserted should come out clean. Do not worry if the custard rises like a soufflé; it will settle when removed from the oven.

6. When done, remove the tart from the oven and place on a cake rack. Let rest for 5 minutes or until the custard settles back.

7. To prepare the optional garnish, preheat the broiler.

8. Cover the top of the tart with the sliced tomatoes, slightly overlapping in a single layer. Brush with 1 tablespoon olive oil. Sprinkle with a good grinding of black pepper and the fresh thyme and rosemary leaves. Place a ring of aluminum foil over the rim of the tart to protect the crust from burning. Place the tart under the broiler, about 6 inches from the source of heat, for

1–2 minutes or until the edges of the tomatoes are lightly browned. Be careful not to burn.

9. Remove the tart from the broiler. Remove the rim of foil and discard. Brush the tomatoes with the remaining tablespoon of olive oil and garnish with the olives. Let the tart stand for 20 minutes or until warm before serving. Serve cut in wedges accompanied by thin slices of hard salami.

R·E·M·A·R·K·S

The tart is equally delicious when served at room temperature.

BASIC TART SHELL

In a food processor bowl, combine 2 cups all-purpose flour, ½ teaspoon salt, and 12 tablespoons unsalted butter, cut into 9 pieces and chilled. Pulse quickly until the mixture resembles oatmeal. Add 3 tablespoons of ice water and pulse quickly until the mixture begins to come together.

By hand, form into a ball, then flatten into a disc, wrap in plastic, and refrigerate for 30 to 40 minutes. Roll into a circle about ⅛ inch thick. Place into the tart pan, trim excess dough, and crimp edges. Prick the bottom of the shell with a fork and chill for 30 minutes.

Preheat the oven to 425°. Line shell with parchment paper, fill with dried beans, and place on a cookie sheet. Place in the center of the oven for 12 minutes. Remove paper and beans and continue to bake for 6 to 8 minutes until dough is set. Place the pan on a wire rack to cool until needed. The tart shell at this point is partially baked.

This recipe is enough for two 9-inch tart pans or one 10-inch quiche dish, with a little bit left over.

BURPEE'S

GARDEN ACCENTS:
RADISHES & SCALLIONS

Along with tender salad greens, radishes are among the first spring crops. Scallions, like chives, are green members of the onion family. In the ways they can be used by the cook, they fall somewhere between an herb and a vegetable. Otherwise unrelated, radishes and scallions have in common their great ability to add flair and flavor to other ingredients. Rarely the centerpiece of a dish on their own, they are distinctive additions to others. Satisfying to grow, radishes and scallions are the favorite accent vegetable from the garden.

RADISHES

As a child, I grew elongated red and white bicolor radishes that were crisp and slightly pungent yet sweet. My mother would serve them, picked fresh from the garden and with but two inches of their tops removed, with black oil-cured olives, crusty bread and fresh sweet butter. To this day I find this snack to be a delightful start to a meal.

Radishes are popular everywhere. In the Near East and the Balkan countries you will find radishes along with cool yogurt and fresh farm cheese served at breakfast. And in Austria and throughout northern Europe, finely sliced black radishes are served with buttered black bread at tastings of young wines. The two-toned radish of my youth (appropriately called French Breakfast radish in the U.S.) is treated with special reverence in France, where farmers bring these tiny jewels to outdoor markets with a prideful reminder that this is the first crop of spring.

In the United States radishes are often taken for granted and always available, even if only in cellophane packages. Thanks to modern transportation and the ever-increasing demand for high-quality produce, you now find truly fresh radishes all over the country.

In spite of the recent efforts of some creative cooks to use radishes as a hot vegetable, the radish is much more interesting raw. The crisp pungent taste of radishes, whether simply sliced,

julienned or cubed, is so good in so many salads that without this little vegetable the spring and fall garden would not be the same.

In the market, look for uniform, firm radishes, preferably with their greens attached. The tops should be crisp and bright green. Avoid radishes that are soft or have yellowish, wilted leaves.

To store radishes, remove their greens and place in a plastic bag in the vegetable bin of the refrigerator; they will easily keep for up to two weeks.

Radishes mature so early—sometimes in only three weeks—that there is hardly an opportunity for anything to go wrong. The most commonly grown types are the round, red roots, such as mild-tasting Cherry Belle, and the all-white roots, such as the round Burpee White and the elongated White Icicle. All these varieties, known as spring radishes, require the cool of spring or autumn. For continuous fresh harvests during these seasons, it is best to sow small plantings (just a few feet of row is enough for most families) about every ten days. I also like to sow radishes between larger, slower-growing crops like cabbage or cauliflower. The tasty roots are ready to pull long before the neighboring crops need the space.

For a heat-resistant radish, try Summer Cross Hybrid, one of the giant white Oriental types known as Daikon. It keeps well and can be stir-fried. Seeds can be sown in midspring for an early summer harvest, or in late summer for a fall harvest. So-called winter radishes, such as Round Black Spanish, require cool weather at the end of their relatively long (55 days) growing season. Plant in summer for a fall harvest.

Although genetic differences among radish varieties are important in determining pungency, the younger the radishes are when picked, the milder they will taste. Roots allowed to remain in the ground too long may become harsh-tasting and pithy.

SCALLIONS

The cultivation of scallions has been perfected to such an extent in the United States that you can now find crisp and uniform bunches with silver-white stalks in most good grocery stores. They also are so easy to grow and so quick to mature that they are planted in most kitchen gardens. There are gardeners who claim that scallions, besides being a wonderful vegetable, will also keep certain pests from nibbling on neighboring crops.

The use of scallions in Western cuisines is essentially confined to the salad bowl. I find their mild taste, lovely green color, and crisp texture a must in an egg, tuna, chicken or rice salad, as well as in most dressings.

In both Japanese and Chinese cooking, scallions are used more than any other member of the onion family except garlic. Oriental cooks use both the white and green parts of the scallion, either chopped, slant-cut, or shredded, in many stir-fries, soups, and noodle dishes. Because of their color, texture, and natural affinity to garlic and ginger, scallions are the perfect garnish to many Oriental dishes. I also use scallions extensively as a base for soups and in several rice dishes.

When preparing this tender young onion, it is best to remove two or three inches of the greens and peel off their outer layer. Once diced, they should be braised in some butter and a touch of broth or water rather than sautéed.

I am frequently asked whether scallions can be used as a substitute for shallots or leeks. They cannot. Although all three belong to the onion family, both leeks and shallots have completely different cooking characteristics and flavors.

Any standard onion variety can be grown as a scallion if harvested early, before the bulbs begin to develop. A convenient space-saving approach is to plant onion sets (small bulbs) or seeds about two inches apart in their rows. When plants reach six inches or more in height, pluck out every other one for use as scallions. The remaining plants are left in the ground, where they will develop into bulbs.

You can also plant Evergreen Long White Bunching onion, which produces excellent stalks but no bulbs. A ten-foot row yields about ten bunches over a month. Seeds can be sown at any time during the season. The plants are hardy enough to winter over in the garden in most climates, although a protective mulch is advisable in the North. When the ground thaws in early spring, simply pull up scallions as your first harvest of the year.

H · A · R · V · E · S · T · I · N · G

Because scallions do not keep very well, it is best to pick them in small quantities as needed.

R · E · C · I · P · E · S

Radish & Snow Pea Salad with Sesame Vinaigrette

P·R·E·P·A·R·A·T·I·O·N

1. In a large serving bowl combine the sesame oil, soy sauce, vinegar, sugar, and peanut oil. Whisk until well blended and set aside.

2. Bring water to a boil in a vegetable steamer, add the snow peas, cover, and steam for 2 minutes. Immediately run cold water to stop further cooking. Drain on paper towels and add to the serving bowl together with the mung bean sprouts, radishes, and scallions. Toss with the sesame vinaigrette and season with salt and pepper. Cover and refrigerate 4–6 hours or overnight.

3. Drain the salad, taste and correct the seasoning, adding a large grinding of black pepper, and serve slightly chilled.

3 tablespoons sesame oil

2 tablespoons soy sauce, preferably thin

3 tablespoons red wine vinegar

1 tablespoon granulated sugar

6 tablespoons peanut oil

6 ounces snow peas, strings removed and cut in half diagonally lengthwise

12 ounces mung bean sprouts (about 6 cups)

2 bunches radishes (about 20–24 medium-sized), trimmed and julienned to equal 2½ cups

4 medium scallions, finely minced

Salt and freshly ground black pepper

SERVES 6

Radish & Beet Salad in Yogurt-Scallion Vinaigrette

1½ pounds cooked beets, peeled and cut into ¾-inch cubes

3 tablespoons olive oil

1 tablespoon red wine vinegar

Salt and freshly ground black pepper

2 cups thinly sliced radishes

3 tablespoons finely minced scallions

2 tablespoons finely minced flat-leaf parsley

1½ cups plain yogurt

SERVES 6

P·R·E·P·A·R·A·T·I·O·N

1. Place the beets in a serving bowl; drizzle with the oil and vinegar and season with salt and pepper to taste. Toss gently to coat the beets and let marinate at room temperature for 1 hour.

2. Add the radishes, scallions, and parsley to the beets. Gently fold in the yogurt, cover, and refrigerate overnight.

3. The next day, bring the salad back to room temperature. Taste and correct the seasoning, adding a generous grinding of black pepper. Serve as an appetizer on a bed of young greens or as an accompaniment to grilled salmon, chicken, or sautéed veal.

Scallion & Buttermilk Pancakes

P·R·E·P·A·R·A·T·I·O·N

1. Sift together the sifted cake flour, baking powder, baking soda, salt, and sugar in a large mixing bowl. Add the egg, buttermilk, and 3 tablespoons melted butter and whisk until well blended. Fold in the scallions and let the batter rest for 1 hour.

2. In a medium skillet heat 2 tablespoons of the butter over medium heat. Add the pancake batter to the skillet by the tablespoonful without crowding the pan. You will have to cook the pancakes in batches, about 6 per batch. Cook until bubbles begin to appear on the surface and bottom is lightly browned. Turn over carefully with a spatula and cook again until lightly browned.

3. Remove from the skillet and transfer to warm individual breakfast plates and sprinkle with freshly ground pepper. Continue to cook more pancakes, adding 2 tablespoons more of butter to the skillet for each batch. After 3 batches, wipe skillet clean with paper towels and begin again. Serve as they come from the skillet with crisp slices of bacon and a poached egg for breakfast or brunch.

R·E·M·A·R·K·S

You may serve the pancakes as an appetizer before a roast leg of lamb or roast pork: Mix together 1 cup sour cream, 2–3 tablespoons finely minced fresh dill, and 2–3 tablespoons red salmon caviar. Season with salt and pepper and top each warm pancake with a bit of the cool sour cream mixture. Garnish with tiny sprigs of fresh dill and a few grains of caviar.

1 cup sifted cake flour
1 teaspoon baking powder
½ teaspoon baking soda
½ teaspoon salt
Pinch of granulated sugar
1 large egg, lightly beaten
1 cup buttermilk
10–12 tablespoons unsalted butter, melted
4 tablespoons finely minced fresh scallions
Freshly ground black pepper

ACCOMPANIMENTS

Slices of crisp meaty bacon
Poached eggs

MAKES 20–24 PANCAKES

Scallion, Potato & Sausage Frittata

P·R·E·P·A·R·A·T·I·O·N

2 tablespoons olive oil

½ pound sweet Italian sausage
(about 3 links)

2 medium russet potatoes, peeled
and thinly sliced

Salt and freshly ground black
pepper

8 large eggs

4 medium scallions, finely minced

2 tablespoons finely minced fresh
parsley

Drops of Tabasco sauce

GARNISH (OPTIONAL)

Tomato Salsa (see Corn Crepes
with Steamed Asparagus &
Spicy Salsa, page 18)

1. Preheat oven to 375°.

2. In a heavy 10-inch skillet, preferably cast iron, heat the olive oil over medium-high heat. Add the sausage and cook quickly until nicely browned on all sides. Remove to a cutting board, cut into ½-inch dice, and reserve.

3. Remove all but 2 tablespoons of fat from the skillet. Add the potato slices, reduce heat, and cook covered for 10 minutes or until tender, turning often in the fat and being careful not to break the slices. Season with salt and pepper, add the diced sausage, and set skillet aside.

4. In a large bowl combine the eggs, scallions, and parsley and whisk until well blended. Season with salt, pepper, and drops of Tabasco.

5. Place the skillet with the potatoes and sausage over medium heat. Add the egg mixture to the skillet and disperse the potatoes and sausages evenly. Cook for 2 minutes until the eggs begin to set on the bottom and are lightly browned. Transfer to the center of the preheated oven and bake for 10–12 minutes or until the eggs are completely set and top has lightly browned.

6. Remove the frittata from the oven and slide onto a serving platter. Serve warm or at room temperature, cut into wedges, with a good spicy Dijon mustard and a well-seasoned green salad.

Spring Salad with Scallion Dressing

P·R·E·P·A·R·A·T·I·O·N

1. Place the mushrooms in a small bowl and sprinkle with lemon juice and a little olive oil. Season with salt and pepper and chill until serving time.

2. In a large shallow salad bowl, combine the mustard, vinegar, remaining olive oil, sugar, salt, and pepper. Whisk until creamy and well blended. Add the scallions and let dressing sit for 30 minutes. Dip each spear of asparagus in the dressing and set aside.

3. Just before serving, whisk the dressing again and top with the lettuces, endives, and beets in the center of the bowl. Divide the asparagus in 4 parts and place at the edge, arranging a strip of pimiento around each section. Sprinkle with minced egg and marinated mushrooms and serve at once.

6 medium fresh mushrooms, wiped, trimmed, and thinly sliced

Juice of ½ lemon

7 tablespoons olive oil

Salt and freshly ground black pepper

2 teaspoons Dijon mustard

2 tablespoons tarragon vinegar

1 teaspoon granulated sugar

3 tablespoons finely minced fresh scallions

12 spears fresh asparagus, trimmed and cooked

1 small head each of Boston lettuce and red leaf lettuce, leaves separated, washed, and dried on paper towels

2 small Belgian endives, cored and quartered lengthwise

2 medium beets, cooked, peeled, and finely cubed

Strips of pimiento (optional)

1 hard-boiled egg, peeled and finely minced

SERVES 4

I · N · D · E · X

SPRING VEGETABLES	WHEN TO PLANT OR SOW FOR SPRING CROP	HOW TO PLANT (SPACING)
ARUGULA	Sow in early spring, then every 2–3 weeks	Seeds: ¼″ deep; thin to 6″ apart in rows 15″ apart
ASPARAGUS	Plant seeds or roots in early to mid-spring	Roots: 1½′ apart in rows 3′ apart
BEETS	Early spring, then every 3 weeks	Seeds: ½″ deep; thin to 3″–4″ apart in rows 1′–2′ apart
BROCCOLI	Sow indoors 6 weeks before last heavy frost; set out plants after last heavy frost	Plant outdoors 15″ apart in rows 2½′ to 3′ apart
COLLARDS	Sow in early spring	Seeds: ¼″ to ½″ deep; thin to 12″–18″ apart in rows 3′ apart
CORN SALAD	Sow in early spring and again 2 weeks later	Seeds: ½″ deep; thin to 6″ apart in rows 1½′ apart
DANDELION	Sow late summer to winter over for early spring crop	Seeds: ¼″ deep; thin to 6″–12″ apart in rows 1½′ apart
KOHLRABI	Early to mid-spring	Seeds: ½″ deep; thin to 3″–4″ apart in rows 1½′ apart
LETTUCE		
BUTTERHEAD TYPES	Start indoors 4–6 weeks before last heavy frost, or outdoors in early spring	Seeds: ½″ deep; thin to 6″–12″ apart in rows 1½′ apart
ENDIVE (CURLY)	Same as Butterhead	Seeds: ½″ deep; thin to 12″ apart in rows 1½′ apart
ICEBERG TYPES	Same as Butterhead	Same as Endive
LOOSEHEAD TYPES	Early spring, then every 2 weeks	Seeds: ½″ deep; thin to 4″–12″ apart in rows 1½′ apart
ROMAINE TYPES	Same as Butterhead	Same as Butterhead
MUSTARD GREENS	Sow in early spring	Seeds: ¼″ deep; thin to 5″ apart in rows 12″–18″ apart
PEAS	Early spring	Seeds: 1″–2″ deep, 1″–2″ apart in double rows 3″ apart; leave 2½′ between double rows
RADISHES	Early spring, then every 7–10 days	Seeds: ½″ deep; thin to 2″ apart in rows 6″ or more apart
SCALLIONS (GREEN ONIONS)	Early spring; or sow in fall for an earlier spring crop	Seeds: ¼″ deep; gradually thin to 1″–2″ apart in rows or 4″ bands each 12″ to 1½′ apart
SORREL	Early spring	Seeds: ½″ deep; thin to 8″ apart in rows 1½′ apart
SPINACH	Early spring	Seeds: ½″ deep; thin to 5″–6″ apart in rows 1½′–2′ apart

Other vegetables often grown as spring garden crops: early cabbage, carrots, cauliflower, Chinese cabbage, kale, rhubarb (a perennial), turnips. Consult your Burpee Gardens catalog for an up-to-date listing of the best varieties for home gardens and for additional planting information.

APPROX. YIELD PER 10' ROW	APPROX. DAYS TO HARVEST	NOTES
5 lbs.	35	Also known as Rocket or Roquette. Pull plants before they go to seed in summer.
Light cutting after one year, 3–4 lbs. each year thereafter	—	Asparagus is a perennial; one planting will yield good stalks for many years.
15 lbs.	53–80	For "baby" beets, use any variety when young, or plant *Little Ball*.
10 lbs.	55–58 *	After large central head is cut, plants develop succulent side shoots for later harvest.
10 lbs.	60	Cut leaves as needed and plants will continue to produce through summer and fall; tolerates heat and frost.
20 plants	30	Also known as *Mâche* or Lamb's Lettuce. Easy to grow.
5 lbs.	—	Pick young leaves; hearts may be blanched by tying outer leaves over centers. Pull plants before they go to seed.
7–8 lbs.	45–60	Best picked when "bulbs" are 2"–3" across.
10–20 heads	75–80	Includes popular Bibb and Boston types.
10 heads	90	Needs long spring season so heads mature before heat of summer.
10 heads	80–90	Needs long spring season so heads mature before heat of summer.
5 lbs. or more	45–50	Easiest lettuce to grow in home gardens.
10–20 heads	83	Indispensable for Caesar salad.
7–10 lbs.	35–40	Easy to grow; very nutritious.
2 lbs. shelled (snap peas much more)	55–74	Snap peas on tall, vigorous vines produce greatest edible yields.
50–60 roots	22–29	Use the common small radishes and Daikon for spring crop; Daikon and other large varieties are for fall crop.
5 lbs.	60	Use any onion seed and pull plants before they form bulbs; or plant *Evergreen Long White Bunching* onion.
5 lbs.	55–70	Sorrel is a perennial; provides greens in early spring for many years.
5 lbs.	39–48	Cut leaves as needed; cut and use entire plant before hot weather causes plants to go to seed.

* From time plants are set out in garden to time of first harvest

A · B · O · U · T · T · H · E · A · U · T · H · O · R

Austrian-born Perla Meyers grew up in Barcelona, Spain, with her Viennese mother and Alsation father. She graduated from the University of Interpreters School and worked for the United Nations in major European cities. In Geneva, she became interested in cooking and food and began intensified study with École Hotelière, the Cordon Blue School, and the Hotel Sacher.

She began her own cooking school in New York in 1960, and now lectures and teaches students how to shop properly and prepare food with a creative attitude. Besides writing best-selling books, appearing on radio and television, and teaching, Ms. Meyers travels throughout Europe visiting markets and working in great restaurants. She lives with her husband and son in New York City and Connecticut.

For more than a century, Burpee has supplied America's gardeners with seeds to grow the tastiest, most productive vegetables and the most beautiful flowers. Burpee's catalogs also feature bulbs, perennial plants, fruit trees, and berries; ornamental nursery stock; and high-quality tools and equipment for all your gardening activities.

Please fill out this form and mail to:

Burpee.

80481 BURPEE BLDG., WARMINSTER, PA 18974

( ) MR.   ( ) MRS.   ( ) MS.

R.R. NO.   BOX NO.

STREET ADDRESS

CITY   STATE   ZIP

CUT HERE

680025

$2

Save $2.00 on Burpee Products!

This coupon is worth $2.00 on

✂ your order of $10.00 or more from any Burpee catalog, *or*

✂ your purchase of $10.00 worth of Burpee seeds and/or Burpee fertilizers at retail stores

TO REDEEM YOUR COUPON:

1. *Burpee Catalog Order:* Just deduct $2.00 from the total amount of your order and enclose this coupon with your order form.

2. *Burpee Retail Purchase:* Write your name and address below and send this coupon with your empty Burpee seed packets (showing color photos and price), or the words "Burpee Fertilizer" cut from the tops of Burpee Fertilizer bottles or bags, or any combination of these products totaling a purchase of $10.00 or more. Store sales receipt must accompany proof-of-purchase. **Mail to Burpee Cookbook Refund Offer, 300 Park Avenue, Warminster, PA 18974.** Please allow 4–6 weeks for receipt of your check.

NAME

ADDRESS

CITY

STATE   ZIP

This coupon is not transferable. No reproductions accepted. Coupon may not be redeemed for cash or exchanged for products at retail stores. Offer void where prohibited by law.

OFFER EXPIRES JUNE 30, 1989

B98012